Legacy Makers

The Legacy Path: Releasing Your Potential in Business and Life

PUBLISHED BY: Adegbuyi Dare Oduguwa

Adegbuyi Oduguwa

Copyright © 2024 All Rights Reserved

No part of this publication may be copied, reproduced in any format, by any means, electronic or otherwise, without prior consent from the copyright owner and publisher of this book.

Table of Contents

Introduction	8
Chapter 1	11
The Ambition Blueprint	11
Part 1: How it all started	11
Part 2: London Arrival	14
Part 3: Discovering His "Why"	17
Principle: Uncovering Your Personal "Why" and Setting Audacious Goals	19
Actionable Takeaways	22
Part 4: Bootstrapping the Start-ups	24
Principle: Building Your Vision and Setting Audacious Goals	26
Actionable Takeaways	28
Chapter 2	31
The Power of Mindset	31
Part 1: The Mindset Shift	31
Principle: The Role of Mindset in Overcoming Challenges	33
Part 2: The Power of Mindset	34
The Fixed vs. Growth Mindset Paradigm	34

Part 3: The Growth Mindset in Action	37
Part 4: Reinventing and Bouncing Back	44
Actionable Takeaways	45
Chapter 3	47
Turning Failure into Innovation	47
Principle: Failure as a Catalyst for Innovation	50
Part 2: The Turning Point	53
The AI-Powered Transformation: Automating Sellapy's Growth	54
The Result: AI as Sellapy's Secret Weapon	59
Actionable Takeaways	62
Chapter 4	64
Leading with Purpose	64
Part 1: Kofo's Leadership Transformation	64
Principle: How Purpose-Driven Leadership Creates Sustainable Success	66
Part 2: Leading the Team with Purpose	69
Part 3: The Power of Partnership - Building Sellapy with Sunshine	71
Principle: Success is Stronger with a Supportive Partner	76
Actionable Takeaways	77

Chapter 5	79
Strategic Risk-Taking for Growth	79
Part 1: The Bold Move That Changed Everything	79
Principle: The Importance of Calculated Risks	82
Part 2: The Leap That Paid Off	84
Part 3: The Bold Gamble That Paid Off – The Birth of SellapyTech	86
The Skyrocket: AI Infrastructure and Scaling Sellapy	89
The Birth of SellapyTech: Monetizing the AI Revolution	91
The Financial Gamble: Business Credit and Other People's Money	93
Actionable Takeaways	94
Chapter 6	97
The Art of Influence and Persuasion	97
Part 1: The Deal That Changed Everything	97
Actionable Takeaways	106
Chapter 7	108
Building High-Performing Teams	108
Principle: How to Build and Sustain a High-Performing Team	110
Part 2: The Turning Point in Team Culture	114

Principle: Sustaining a High-Performing Team	115
Actionable Takeaways	117
Chapter 8	120
Time Mastery and Balance	120
Part 1: The Breaking Point	120
Principle: The Importance of Time Management and Balance	122
Part 2: The Shift Toward Balance	125
Principle: Balance Is Essential for Sustainable Success	127
Part 3: A Taste of the Billionaire Life – The Private Island Escape	129
Principle: Hard Work Pays Off, But Don't Forget to Celebrate	134
Actionable Takeaways	136
Chapter 9	139
Embracing Change and Disruption	139
Part 1: The Disruption That Nearly Derailed It All	139
Principle: How to Turn Disruption Into Opportunity	141
Part 2: The Pivot That Saved the Day	143
Part 3: Sellapy's Disruptive Innovation	147
Actionable Takeaways	148

Chapter 10 150

Creating a Lasting Legacy 150

Part 1: The Legacy Conversation That Changed Everything 150

Principle: Building a Legacy That Lasts Beyond Success 152

Part 2: The Moment of Stepping Back 155

Principle: Legacy Is About More Than Success 156

Part 3: The Philanthropy Plan That Touched Millions 159

Principle: Legacy Through Sustainable Impact 166

Actionable Takeaways 168

The Final Revelation: A Vision from the Present into the Future 171

Summary of the Chapters 175

Acknowledgements 180

Legacy Makers 182

Introduction

Every empire begins with a dream, a spark of ambition, a glimmer of something larger than ourselves. For as long as I can remember, I've had that dream. It wasn't always clear, nor did I always know how I would achieve it. But deep down, I knew I was destined to build something that mattered, something that would last long after I was gone.

I wasn't born into wealth or privilege. In fact, my journey began far from the bustling business hubs and investment capital networks that many successful entrepreneurs call home. I grew up in **Nigeria**, surrounded by resilience, but also by the harsh realities of life for those without access to opportunities. Like so many others, I saw the hunger, the struggle, and the systemic barriers that kept dreams small and survival at the forefront.

But I was determined that **my story** would be different. And not just for me, my journey would be a testament to what can happen when you refuse to let circumstances define you. The success I dreamed of wasn't just for myself; it was for the countless others like me who had ambition but lacked resources, for the dreamers who wanted to build something but didn't know where to begin.

Sellapy, **SellapyTech**, and the vision for **Sellapy Farms** were born from that desire, not just to succeed, but to **empower**. This book isn't about building businesses for the sake of profit alone. It's about creating **impact**, about turning personal ambition into something far greater: a **legacy**.

What is a legacy? It's the thing that remains when we're no longer here. The mark we leave on the world, the lives we change, and the systems we transform. In this book, I share the real and raw journey of building a global empire, alongside my partner Sunshine, and the lessons we've learned along the way. From the early failures to the triumphs that followed, you'll see how we transformed our dreams into **vehicles of change**, for ourselves, our communities, and the world.

Whether you're an entrepreneur, a professional looking for purpose, or someone who wants to leave a meaningful mark on the world, this book is for you. **"Legacy Makers"** is about more than just business, it's about finding your **why**, navigating adversity, and using your success to **uplift others**.

Our journey hasn't been easy, but every challenge has made us stronger, more innovative, and more committed to the vision of creating something **lasting**. And now, I invite you to join me on this path to build, to dream, and to craft your own **legacy**.

Seat back and enjoy every line of the story.

Chapter 1

The Ambition Blueprint

Part 1: How it all started

It was the heat that he remembered most clearly from those early days in Lagos. The kind of oppressive, sticky heat that clung to your skin no matter how many times you wiped your brow. **Kofo**, a 24-year-old man from a modest family, sat outside his small one-room apartment. His parents were both teachers, respected in their community, but living modestly, barely making ends meet. Kofo had ambition. Though, something that was bigger than the heat, bigger than the chaos of Lagos, and much bigger than the expectations placed on him.

He had always known that there was more to life than the limitations his environment imposed. Growing up, he watched his friends fall into the traps of quick money schemes or become consumed by the frustrations of discrimination and lack of opportunity. Some had resorted to illegal means, their lives spiralling into the shadowy underworld of scamming, drugs, and violence. He had seen others give in to despair, believing the world was against them, believing that success was not for people like them.

But Kofo? He refused to be distracted by the noise.

With each passing day, he felt the pull of his ambition. It was a quiet but relentless force, urging him to push beyond the boundaries of what people expected from a young man in his position. His dreams weren't defined by where he was born, nor were they bound by the limitations of his background. He knew he was destined for more, and he decided that it would be through legitimate, hard-earned success.

Kofo's ambition was to create something that would last—something bigger than himself. But he knew he needed a change of environment to make that happen. The opportunities around him in Lagos were slim, and even though he had graduated with a degree in Computer Science from a local university, job offers were sparse. Every day felt like a fight against the tide.

So, he made a bold decision: he would pursue a new life in London, despite knowing the odds were against him. He didn't have a visa yet, nor did he have family waiting for him there. All he had was a distant cousin who had moved to the UK years earlier and a deep belief that if he worked hard enough, he could carve out a new path.

Getting a visa wasn't easy. He spent months saving, taking on odd jobs, and spending every last naira to navigate the complex and costly immigration process. He worked as a part-time IT assistant during the day, and in the evenings, he helped out at his uncle's small grocery shop, often for little more than a meal. Every day felt long and gruelling, but he was determined. He avoided the negative voices around him—those that told him that it was impossible, or that success could only come through dishonest means. He also stayed away from the scammers who promised "shortcuts" to getting abroad quickly.

Instead, Kofo put his head down and worked. He built up a small fund, just enough to pay for his visa application and a one-way ticket to London. He had no idea what awaited him on the other side, but he believed that if he could just make it to London, he could work his way up to success, brick by brick.

"Your background may shape your path, but it doesn't define your destination. True ambition is born when you dare to dream beyond your circumstances."

Part 2: London Arrival

When Kofo finally landed in London, it wasn't the shiny, glamorous metropolis he had envisioned. It was cold and unwelcoming, the sky a constant shade of grey. But he hadn't come for comfort; he had come to work.

With nothing but a few hundred pounds in his pocket, he immediately took up a job as a construction labourer. He didn't mind that it wasn't in his field of study. He knew that every hard day on the construction site was a stepping stone toward his greater ambition. His first weeks were spent hauling bricks, mixing cement, and working under supervisors who barely noticed him. The hours were long and exhausting, but Kofo worked harder than anyone. He learned quickly that London was a city that rewarded hustle, and no matter how many times his body ached from physical labour, he refused to quit.

In between shifts, he would use whatever spare time he had to apply for better jobs, particularly in IT, his area of expertise. But breaking into that world wasn't easy. As a Nigerian immigrant, he often felt like he had to work twice as hard just to get noticed. His applications were frequently rejected without explanation. Discrimination was something he had anticipated, but he had made a pact with himself long ago—he would never let it define his journey. Racism, stereotypes, and bias were real, but they were just another obstacle to overcome, not a reason to give up.

Kofo's first break came when he landed a job as a kitchen porter in a high-end restaurant in Central London. The work was brutal, washing dishes for hours on end, but it paid lesser than construction, and he saw it as an opportunity to learn the language of business from a different angle. He was surrounded by people who worked their way up in the hospitality industry, and he began to network, making small but valuable connections. He learned the value of resilience in a city that rewarded perseverance.

After six months of relentless work, Kofo saved enough to take an online course in IT. Every penny he earned went toward advancing his skills, and slowly but surely, doors began to open. He took on freelance IT projects, offering his services to small businesses that couldn't afford large tech firms. It wasn't glamorous, but it was progress.

Kofo's next breakthrough came when he landed his first real IT job as an engineer for a small company in East London. This was the moment he had been waiting for—a foot in the door of the tech world. But even then, he knew this wasn't the end. His real ambition was to start his own company, to build something from the ground up.

With each step, Tunde bootstrapped his way forward, refusing to give in to the temptations of quick success through illegal means. His story wasn't about shortcuts; it was about grit, vision, and unwavering focus on his long-term goals.

"Success is not about where you start, but how relentlessly you push forward—one brick, one challenge, one opportunity at a time."

Part 3: Discovering His "Why"

As Kofo began to settle into his IT job, he noticed something interesting. The more he worked in the industry, the more he realized that the problems small businesses faced with technology were often the same. Many lacked the resources or knowledge to integrate even basic IT solutions, and as a result, they were held back. For Kofo, this wasn't just a job anymore, it became a mission. He could see the gap between the technology that existed and the small businesses that needed it most, especially immigrant-owned businesses that, like him, were working to get a foothold in a fast-paced, competitive world.

This realization sparked something deep inside him. He began to ask himself, **"Why am I really doing this? What impact do I want to have?"** It wasn't enough for him to simply work a job and pay his bills. He had always believed in something bigger, something that would allow him to give back to the community and solve real problems.

Kofo started to reflect on his journey: how he had navigated countless rejections, the feeling of isolation, and the weight of discrimination. Yet, he had managed to rise above those challenges, staying true to his principles and refusing to take unethical shortcuts. His why wasn't just about making money, it was about **empowering others** who, like him, were navigating life as immigrants, fighting to break through barriers and find their own path to success.

He realized that his true ambition was not just about succeeding for himself, but about **creating opportunities for others**. The tech industry had given him a lifeline, and he wanted to extend that to people and businesses who were still struggling. This became his **core mission**: to build an IT consulting company that specifically catered to the needs of small, immigrant-owned businesses, helping them integrate the latest technology, grow, and compete on a level playing field.

But Kofo knew this wouldn't be easy. Starting a business from scratch in a city like London, without significant funding or connections, was an uphill battle. The temptation to give up or to settle for a stable IT job was always there, but Kofo's why, the burning desire to create a positive impact and help others, kept him focused. He knew that if he could succeed, it would be a victory for more than just himself; it would be a model for others who believed their circumstances were holding them back.

Kofo's journey was about more than entrepreneurship, it was about **ambition with purpose**. His vision became clearer each day: he wasn't just bootstrapping a business to make a profit; he was building a legacy that could inspire others to follow in his footsteps, to rise above their challenges, and to find success through hard work, integrity, and resilience.

Principle: Uncovering Your Personal "Why" and Setting Audacious Goals

Kofo's story is not unique in the challenges he faced, but it's extraordinary in how he turned those challenges into fuel for his ambition. At the heart of every successful individual or business is a deep-rooted **why**, a purpose that drives every decision, even when the odds seem insurmountable. Finding your why is the foundation for building a life and career that is not only successful but also fulfilling.

In this section, we will explore how **uncovering your personal why** can give you clarity and direction, even when external circumstances try to pull you off course. Whether you're an aspiring entrepreneur, a professional seeking career growth, or someone looking to make a change, your why is your compass.

1. **Reflect on Your Journey**: Take a moment to reflect on your life experiences. What are the challenges you've faced, and what have they taught you? Often, our greatest struggles give birth to our most meaningful ambitions. Tunde's journey from Lagos to London wasn't just about survival; it was about proving that his background wouldn't define his future.
2. **Ask the Big Questions**: Why do you want to succeed? What drives you beyond the desire for financial stability or status? For Kofo, it was about helping others who were navigating the same challenges he had faced. Your why should go deeper than external rewards—it should connect to something that makes you feel passionate and fulfilled.

3. **Connect Your Why to Your Ambition**: Once you've identified your why, it's time to connect it to your goals. Ambition without purpose can feel hollow, but when your goals are aligned with your core beliefs, every step forward feels meaningful. Tunde didn't just want to be an entrepreneur; he wanted to **solve real problems** for underserved businesses. This purpose gave him the determination to keep pushing through adversity.

4. **Set Audacious, Purpose-Driven Goals**: Ambition thrives when it's paired with bold, audacious goals. It's not enough to aim for what feels safe or attainable; true growth happens when you push yourself beyond what you believe is possible. Tunde could have settled for a comfortable IT job, but he set his sights higher. He envisioned creating a company that would not only provide for him but also lift up other small businesses.

5. **Stay Focused on the Long Game**: Success rarely happens overnight. It's easy to get discouraged when progress seems slow, but when your goals are aligned with your purpose, the journey becomes just as important as the destination. Kofo's journey from construction labourer to IT engineer and eventually entrepreneur wasn't linear. It was full of setbacks and challenges, but his ambition and purpose kept him moving forward.

Actionable Takeaways

At the end of this chapter, readers will learn that ambition without purpose is hollow, and setting audacious, purpose-driven goals is essential to building lasting success. Here are three actionable steps to help you uncover your why and set bold goals:

1. **Define Your Core Purpose**: Take 15 minutes to write down your top five life experiences that have shaped who you are today. Reflect on how those experiences connect to what truly drives you.
2. **Create Your Vision Board**: Using your core purpose, craft a vision board that illustrates what success looks like to you in five years. This will help

you visualize your goals and keep your ambition aligned with your why.

3. **Set Audacious Goals with Milestones**: Choose three bold, long-term goals that feel slightly out of reach. Break these down into smaller milestones, and make a commitment to work toward them daily, no matter how incremental the progress.

"When you find your 'why,' every obstacle becomes a stepping stone, and every setback turns into fuel for your purpose-driven ambition."

In the next part, we'll explore the **importance of mindset**, drawing from Kofo's ongoing journey. While ambition is the spark, mindset is the fuel that keeps the flame burning—especially when the road gets tough.

Part 4: Bootstrapping the Start-ups

With his IT job providing a stable foundation, **Kofo** began working on his long-term vision: becoming an entrepreneur who could empower others, particularly small businesses that struggled to scale. He knew first-hand how difficult it was to break through barriers, especially as an immigrant with limited resources. The solution became clear to him: create platforms and services that would **enable small and medium-sized enterprises (SMEs)** to thrive in both local and global markets. But this wouldn't be just another entrepreneurial venture, it would be a mission-driven business focused on solving real problems.

The first idea that came to Kofo was **Sellapy**, a comprehensive **eCommerce marketplace** designed to help SMEs buy and sell goods locally and internationally. He had seen the struggles of small businesses, especially those run by immigrant entrepreneurs, who lacked access to global markets due to high fees and complex logistics. Sellapy would remove those barriers, offering an intuitive, low-cost platform that allowed anyone to sell their products globally, without the need for advanced tech skills or large budgets.

Bootstrapping Sellapy was no easy task. Kofo knew he didn't have access to large capital or big investors, so he focused on **lean growth** strategies. He started small, testing the marketplace with a few vendors, and then scaled it step by step. To fund the initial stages, he saved every penny from his IT salary and took on freelance work during the evenings. His days were long, filled with client meetings, technical development, and website optimization. But every sale that went through Sellapy felt like a personal victory, confirming that there was a real demand for the marketplace.

Once Sellapy gained traction and began turning a profit, Kofo's entrepreneurial vision expanded. He realized that eCommerce businesses, especially those on Sellapy, faced another common issue: keeping up with modern technology. Many businesses lacked the resources to build effective websites or use artificial intelligence to optimize their operations. That's when **SellapyTech** was born, a **technology solutions business** focused on providing AI-driven services, such as **building websites** and developing **AI-powered customer service agents** for retail and eCommerce companies.

Kofo's goal with SellapyTech was simple: to **democratise access to cutting-edge technology**. He wanted small businesses to have the same tools as the big players, enabling them to compete on a global stage. He developed AI solutions that were easy to implement and cost-effective, making them accessible to businesses that couldn't otherwise afford high-end tech solutions.

Principle: Building Your Vision and Setting Audacious Goals

Kofo's journey illustrates an important principle for any aspiring entrepreneur: **your ambition should always be matched by a bold, long-term vision**. Whether you're starting a marketplace like Sellapy or a tech solution like SellapyTech, it's critical to think beyond short-term success. Kofo wasn't just building businesses—he was creating platforms that could change the landscape for small businesses worldwide.

Here's how you can apply this principle in your own life:
1. **Start with a Mission**: Like Kofo, your business should solve a real problem. In his case, it was the difficulty that small businesses faced in accessing

global markets and cutting-edge technology. Ask yourself, what problem can you solve that will have a meaningful impact on your target audience? What drives you to keep pushing forward, even when resources are limited?

2. **Set Audacious Goals**: Your goals should be so big that they scare you a little. Kofo's vision for Sellapy wasn't just about local eCommerce, it was about creating a global marketplace for SMEs, which meant competing with major players. He could have aimed lower, but by setting ambitious goals, he gave himself a reason to stay motivated, even when things got tough.

3. **Bootstrap Your Way to Success**: One of Kofo's greatest strengths was his ability to start small and scale as resources allowed. He didn't wait for investors or huge sums of money to come his way. Instead, he used his skills, saved diligently, and leveraged freelance work to fund his startups. You don't always need large amounts of capital to begin; sometimes, you just need determination and a strategic approach to growth.

4. **Embrace Technology Early**: Kofo's pivot to SellapyTech was a game-changer for his business

and the clients he served. By incorporating AI-driven solutions, he ensured that his platform was at the forefront of innovation. In today's world, technology is a critical driver of success. Whatever your industry, find ways to leverage the latest tech to provide greater value to your customers.

Actionable Takeaways

Here are three practical steps you can take from Kofo's entrepreneurial journey:

1. **Define Your Audacious Vision**: Take time to reflect on the broader impact you want your business or career to have. What is your five-year vision, and how will your work impact your customers, industry, or community? Write this down, and revisit it regularly to stay focused on your big-picture goals.

2. **Bootstrap Your Business**: If you're starting with limited funds, map out a strategy to fund your venture with existing resources. Identify freelance work, side gigs, or partnerships that can help you gather initial capital without taking on debt or relying on external investors. Remember, Kofo built Sellapy and SellapyTech without waiting for big

investment; he bootstrapped it through hard work and resourcefulness.

3. **Leverage AI and Tech**: If you're running a business, find ways to integrate technology early in your operations. Research tools that can help automate tasks, optimize customer service, or improve the user experience. AI is no longer just for large corporations—there are scalable solutions for small and medium-sized businesses. SellapyTech made AI accessible to small eCommerce businesses, and you can do the same in your industry.

Kofo's entrepreneurial path rooted in his why, focused on solving real problems, and powered by ambition serves as a powerful model for anyone looking to create lasting success. But ambition and strategy alone aren't enough. In the next chapter, we'll explore how **mindset mastery** plays a crucial role in overcoming adversity and building resilience, just as Kofo did when he navigated the challenges of launching his startups in a competitive environment.

Adegbuyi Oduguwa

"Building something great doesn't require shortcuts or shortcuts to capital—it requires vision, grit, and the courage to start where you are with what you have."

Chapter 2

The Power of Mindset

Part 1: The Mindset Shift

As Kofo's startups began to gain traction, he faced challenges that were far more complex than just building a business from the ground up. The roadblocks weren't only financial or technical—they were mental. He realized that running Sellapy and SellapyTech required more than just hustle and strategy. It demanded a mindset that could withstand failure, uncertainty, and the inevitable moments of doubt that creep in when success doesn't come as fast as expected.

Kofo's first real mental challenge came during the early stages of launching SellapyTech. After months of building relationships and developing AI-driven solutions, the company landed a contract with a promising retail chain in East London. This contract was supposed to be the breakthrough, the kind of deal that would put SellapyTech on the map and lead to a series of future projects.

But, like many entrepreneurs, Kofo soon learned that success in business is never a straight line. Just two months into the project, the retail chain's investors pulled out, leaving Kofo with a partial payment and a mountain of work still to be completed. Worse, he had already hired new developers and invested in additional resources, expecting this contract to open more doors.

For most, this kind of setback would have been devastating. Kofo felt the familiar pull of doubt. Had he miscalculated? Should he have stayed with his stable IT job? Was he in over his head? It would have been easy to feel defeated, to focus on the losses and retreat back into a safer career.

But Kofo wasn't the same person who had landed in London years ago. This time, he recognized that setbacks were part of the entrepreneurial journey. He understood that his response to failure was what would truly define his path.

In that moment, Kofo made a critical decision: **he would reframe the setback not as a failure, but as a learning opportunity.** It was time to put his growth mindset into practice. Rather than dwell on the loss of the contract, he shifted his focus to the lessons he could extract from the experience. What had gone wrong? What could he have done differently? And most importantly, how could he use this as fuel to improve his business?

Principle: The Role of Mindset in Overcoming Challenges

Kofo's journey is a testament to the transformative power of a **growth mindset**. In life and business, there are two kinds of mindsets: **the fixed mindset** and **the growth mindset**. People with a fixed mindset believe that their abilities and intelligence are static, while those with a growth mindset understand that abilities can be developed through dedication and effort.

Kofo adopted the growth mindset early in his career, recognizing that failure wasn't something to be feared—it was something to be **learned from.** This mental shift became one of his greatest strengths as an entrepreneur.

Part 2: The Power of Mindset

The Fixed vs. Growth Mindset Paradigm

The difference between a **fixed mindset** and a **growth mindset** can be transformative in business and life. Kofo's success wasn't just the result of hard work; it was his mental approach to challenges that defined his journey. To understand how this played a crucial role, it's important to explore these two types of mindsets in practical terms.

1. **Fixed Mindset**: A fixed mindset is the belief that one's abilities, intelligence, and talents are static—unchangeable traits that people are either born with or without. Individuals with a fixed mindset often avoid challenges, give up easily, and view effort as fruitless because they believe their capabilities are fixed.

   Imagine a young entrepreneur named **Bola** who, like Kofo, dreamed of starting her own tech company. She landed her first big project but, after a few months, the project faced major setbacks. Bola began to feel that maybe she wasn't cut out for entrepreneurship after all. In her mind, if the project failed, it was a reflection of her innate abilities. She believed that if she were truly talented, success would have come more easily. So, rather than finding solutions, she began to withdraw, eventually giving up on her venture entirely.

This is the danger of a fixed mindset. It leads to stagnation because the individual believes they've reached their limits. There's no room for growth because they view their skills as fixed and unchangeable.

2. **Growth Mindset**: On the other hand, a growth mindset is the belief that abilities can be developed through dedication, learning, and hard work. Setbacks aren't seen as failures but as opportunities to grow, adapt, and improve. People with a growth mindset embrace challenges, persist in the face of adversity, and see effort as the path to mastery. When Kofo faced a major setback with the retail chain pulling out of their contract with SellapyTech, he could have easily fallen into the trap of a fixed mindset. It would have been easy to think, *"Maybe I'm not as good at this as I thought. Maybe I'm not meant to succeed as an entrepreneur."* Instead, Kofo leaned into his growth mindset. He asked himself: *"What can I learn from this? How can I use*

this challenge to improve my business model?" By doing so, he identified new opportunities and pivoted his business to target smaller clients. He didn't view the setback as a reflection of his abilities; he saw it as a necessary part of the learning process.

"Your mindset is the filter through which you see challenges—either as threats that limit you or as opportunities that grow you."

Part 3: The Growth Mindset in Action

Let's dive deeper into how Kofo applied his **growth mindset** during pivotal moments in his journey, and how adopting this mindset can lead to innovative thinking and problem-solving.

1. **Embracing Challenges Rather than Avoiding Them**: Kofo's initial venture into the world of entrepreneurship wasn't easy. When Sellapy was still in its infancy, there were times when he doubted himself. Building an eCommerce marketplace from the ground up required far more than technical skills; it required resilience, creativity, and the ability to **embrace challenges** head-on.

One challenge came when Kofo realized that to expand Sellapy globally, he would need to compete with large eCommerce platforms with far more resources. Many people in Kofo's position would have hesitated or even given up. They might have thought, *"There's no way I can compete with these giant companies. I'll never have the funding or the team to grow at that scale."* This is a classic **fixed mindset**, where fear of competition leads to avoidance.

But Kofo, with his growth mindset, took a different approach. He **embraced the challenge**, recognizing that his smaller size could actually work in his favour. While the larger companies were slow-moving and bureaucratic, Sellapy could be agile and customer-focused, addressing the needs of small businesses in ways that bigger companies couldn't. He leveraged this competitive advantage to offer personalized services and solutions, carving out a unique niche for his business.

2. **Viewing Effort as the Path to Mastery**: A fixed mindset often leads people to believe that if something requires too much effort, it's not worth pursuing. They assume that talent and intelligence should come naturally and that hard work is a sign of inadequacy. But **Kofo viewed effort as the pathway to mastery**.

In the early days of **SellapyTech**, Kofo put in long hours not just to keep the business running but to continually improve his skills. He spent nights learning about the latest developments in **artificial intelligence** and **eCommerce technologies**, understanding that staying on the cutting edge would give him a competitive edge. He also took on freelance work to fund his business, even when it meant less sleep and more stress.

Rather than seeing effort as an obstacle, Kofo saw it as the necessary fuel for success. He understood that **growth requires sustained effort**, and he was willing to put in that effort, even when the immediate results weren't visible.

Contrast this with a tech entrepreneur named **James**. After experiencing several months of difficulty building his AI solution, James began to believe that maybe the AI industry wasn't for him. He saw other entrepreneurs succeeding faster and assumed they must be naturally more talented or smarter than he was. Instead of persisting, he gave up and shifted to an easier project. This is where the fixed mindset limits potential. By avoiding effort, James denied himself the opportunity to grow into the successful entrepreneur he could have been.

3. **Learning from Criticism**: Early in SellapyTech's journey, Kofo received feedback from several of his clients. They appreciated his AI solutions but felt that the user interface of his products was too complex for smaller businesses. Rather than

becoming defensive—a common trait in those with a fixed mindset—Kofo took this criticism to heart. He saw it as an opportunity to **improve and refine** his offerings.

He hired a UI/UX expert to help redesign the platform, making it more intuitive for non-technical users. This change not only improved customer satisfaction but also increased the number of clients who were willing to adopt his AI solutions. By embracing constructive criticism, Kofo used it as a catalyst for growth, transforming a potential weakness into one of his company's greatest strengths. In contrast, imagine an entrepreneur named **Susan**, whose tech product received negative feedback from its early users. Instead of using that feedback to improve, Susan became defensive, believing that her product was already perfect. She refused to make any changes, convinced that the customers just "didn't get it." Over time, her refusal to adapt led to her product being overshadowed by competitors who were more open to feedback and continuous improvement.

4. **Persevering Through Setbacks**: Kofo's journey wasn't without its share of setbacks. But every time he encountered a hurdle, his growth mindset helped him to keep pushing forward. Whether it was the lost retail contract or the slow early adoption of Sellapy, he viewed every setback as **temporary** and as an opportunity to **learn**. Instead of retreating, he leaned in, finding solutions and adjusting his strategies.

This kind of perseverance is what separates those who eventually succeed from those who give up too early. Kofo knew that building something worthwhile would take time, and he was willing to **embrace the journey**, knowing that each setback was just another step toward eventual success.

Here's how Kofo applied the principles of mindset mastery to overcome challenges and create lasting success:

1. **Failure is a Teacher, Not a Threat**: When the retail chain contract fell through, Kofo could have seen it as a personal failure, a sign that his business wasn't viable. Instead, he chose to view it as feedback—valuable data that would help him refine his approach. The growth mindset allowed him to distance himself from the failure, recognizing that it wasn't an indictment of his abilities but an opportunity to improve.

2. **Resilience Through Reframing**: Challenges are inevitable in entrepreneurship. What defines successful entrepreneurs is their ability to reframe those challenges in a way that fuels progress rather than halts it. Kofo's resilience wasn't about ignoring the difficulty of his situation, it was about using his mindset to reframe setbacks as temporary and solvable, not permanent and insurmountable.

3. **Continuous Learning is the Key to Growth**: One of the core tenets of the growth mindset is the belief that **learning never stops**. Even as Kofo gained more experience, he never assumed he had "arrived." Every challenge, every failure, and every

success became an opportunity to learn and adapt. This mindset allowed him to keep evolving as an entrepreneur, ensuring that both Sellapy and SellapyTech stayed innovative and competitive.

4. **Embrace Uncertainty**: Kofo learned to thrive in uncertain conditions. As a bootstrapped entrepreneur, he didn't have the luxury of guaranteed success, but he did have control over his mindset. Rather than fear uncertainty, Kofo embraced it, knowing that discomfort was often a sign of growth.

"Success isn't about avoiding failure; it's about embracing each setback as the fuel for your next breakthrough."

Part 4: Reinventing and Bouncing Back

After the initial setback with the retail chain, Kofo made an important decision. Instead of retreating or downsizing, he chose to **pivot**. He reached out to smaller businesses—those who were eager to use AI solutions but couldn't afford the big tech firms. These were the underdogs, just like he had been. His growth mindset made him adaptable, allowing him to shift his target market without abandoning his long-term vision.

Kofo restructured SellapyTech's offerings, creating scalable packages that were more affordable for small and medium-sized businesses. This pivot led to several new contracts with businesses that valued his company's innovative approach and hands-on support. Within six months, Kofo's business was back on track, and the failure with the retail chain had become nothing more than a small hiccup on his way to bigger successes.

What could have been a devastating blow to Kofo's business turned into a growth opportunity, thanks to his mindset. He didn't let the setback define him or his business. Instead, he used it to **reinvent his strategy** and grow even stronger.

Actionable Takeaways

Here are three practical steps to help you adopt a growth mindset and overcome the inevitable challenges you'll face on your path to success:

1. **Reframe Failures as Lessons**: Whenever you experience a setback, write down what you can learn from the situation. Ask yourself, "What went wrong, and how can I improve?" Make a habit of viewing failures as opportunities for growth, rather than as dead ends.

2. **Practice Resilience**: Setbacks are inevitable, but resilience is a skill you can develop. When challenges arise, take a moment to breathe, assess the situation, and refocus on your long-term vision. Don't let short-term difficulties derail your bigger ambitions.

3. **Commit to Continuous Learning**: Never stop learning. Whether through formal education, mentorship, or self-study, make learning a part of your daily routine. The most successful people are those who embrace the idea that there's always room for growth and improvement.

Kofo's transformation into a resilient entrepreneur, capable of bouncing back from adversity, was driven by his growth mindset. The lesson here is clear: if you can master your mindset, you can master your future. No matter what challenges come your way, the growth mindset will allow you to navigate them with confidence and resilience.

"The true measure of success is not how you avoid failure, but how you reinvent yourself every time you rise from it."

In the next chapter, we'll explore **how failure can be used as a tool for innovation**. Kofo's journey isn't just about overcoming setbacks—it's about using those setbacks as fuel to innovate and create even greater success.

Chapter 3

Turning Failure into Innovation

Part 1: The Sellapy Marketplace Pivot

Kofo stood in his small, makeshift office, staring at the data on his laptop. Less than fifty users in a year. After months of grinding, pushing, and promoting **Sellapy**, the results were disheartening. The vision he had for the **Sellapy marketplace**—a platform for micro-businesses in developing countries to sell their products globally—hadn't materialised as he had hoped.

Kofo had poured everything into this idea. He had envisioned the app as a tool that would empower small business owners in places like Nigeria, Kenya, and Bangladesh to reach customers across the globe. He believed that the platform could help lift communities out of poverty by connecting them to global markets. But the numbers didn't lie: Sellapy had failed to find product-market fit.

The app had less than fifty users, and engagement was minimal. After a full year, the dream he had worked tirelessly to build felt like it was slipping away. Kofo had to make a decision. He could either cut his losses and shut down the marketplace or **pivot**, rethinking the entire business model. But as disheartening as the failure was, Kofo wasn't ready to quit. He believed in the core idea—there was just something missing.

After analysing user data, customer feedback, and market trends, Kofo decided to shift the focus of Sellapy toward **eco-friendly products**. He had noticed a growing global demand for sustainability and ethical products, and he thought Sellapy could serve as a marketplace for these items, providing a platform for eco-conscious consumers to connect with businesses offering sustainable solutions. This pivot seemed promising, and for a while, it looked like the new version of Sellapy might succeed.

But then came another blow.

Technical issues plagued the platform from day one. The developers Kofo had hired to build the new version of the app fell behind schedule, introduced bugs, and ultimately delivered a product that was unstable and riddled with errors. Customers who had initially signed up for the eco-friendly marketplace started leaving in droves. Defects in the platform's functionality made it nearly impossible to retain users. Within months, Kofo's user base dwindled again, and the second iteration of Sellapy collapsed.

Still, Kofo didn't give up. He knew the idea had potential—it just needed the right execution. This time, he decided to pivot again, but the challenges didn't stop there. The third version of Sellapy faced even bigger hurdles: **funding constraints** and an inability to build a **marketing team**. Without adequate capital and the right people to promote the platform, Sellapy struggled to gain visibility. Kofo found himself once again staring down the barrel of potential failure.

But for Kofo, failure wasn't the end—it was a signal that something needed to change. He understood that setbacks were opportunities in disguise, and with every failure, he learned something valuable about his market, his product, and himself.

Principle: Failure as a Catalyst for Innovation

Kofo's experience with Sellapy is a perfect example of how **failure can be used as a tool for innovation**. Many entrepreneurs see failure as the end of the road, but Kofo saw it as part of the process, an opportunity to pivot, innovate, and evolve.

Here's how Kofo turned each failure into a stepping stone for future success:

1. **Analyse the Failure, Don't Dwell on It**

    Kofo didn't just give up when the first iteration of Sellapy failed to attract users. Instead of seeing the low user count as a personal failure, he took a step back and analysed what had gone wrong. He understood that the product-market fit was off, micro-businesses in developing countries didn't have the infrastructure or consistent internet access to fully utilize the platform. Rather than dwell on what hadn't worked, Kofo focused on gathering data, understanding his customers better, and identifying market gaps.

2. **Pivot with Purpose**

   When Kofo shifted Sellapy to focus on eco-friendly products, it wasn't a random decision. He had identified a growing trend in sustainable consumerism and saw an opportunity to target a niche that was gaining momentum. Pivoting isn't just about changing direction; it's about doing so **with purpose**, based on evidence, trends, and customer feedback. While the second iteration of Sellapy didn't succeed due to technical issues, the pivot itself was a smart, calculated move based on market needs.

3. **Embrace Technical and Operational Setbacks as Learning Experiences**

   The technical issues Kofo faced with his developers during the eco-friendly phase were devastating at the time, but they taught him an important lesson about **quality control** and the need to vet technical teams thoroughly. He realized that no matter how good an idea is, execution matters. In the future, Kofo became much more meticulous in selecting developers, ensuring that the technical infrastructure of his businesses was solid before launching. Each technical failure wasn't a dead end—it was a lesson in how to better manage teams, projects, and expectations.

4. **Funding and Marketing Constraints Force Creativity**

When Kofo faced funding challenges in the third iteration of Sellapy, he realized that **constraints can drive innovation**. Without the budget to hire a full marketing team, Kofo had to get creative. He began focusing on low-cost marketing strategies, leveraging social media platforms, influencer marketing, and partnerships with other small businesses. While this wasn't the ideal situation, it forced him to think outside the box and develop cost-effective ways to promote Sellapy. These strategies later became part of Sellapy's DNA, allowing the platform to grow sustainably without relying on massive advertising budgets.

"Failure isn't the end of the road—it's a detour that leads you to the path of innovation."

Part 2: The Turning Point

By the time Kofo launched the **third iteration of Sellapy**, he had learned from each previous failure. He knew that if the platform was going to succeed, it had to be built on a **solid foundation**, one that combined a clear product-market fit, robust technology, and a lean, efficient marketing strategy. This time, it was about **empowering small businesses** globally in a way no other platform had done before. It was no longer just an idea—it had evolved into a **mission**. Kofo wanted to build a marketplace that truly levelled the playing field, where **local SMEs, artisans, and niche vendors** could access global markets without the barriers that had held them back for so long.

This version of Sellapy was built for the **underdogs**—the businesses in remote towns, the artisans crafting unique products in small workshops, the niche vendors whose local appeal had yet to reach the world stage. Kofo knew that these businesses had immense potential, but they were often left out of the global commerce conversation. They lacked the infrastructure for cross-border payments, faced high shipping costs, and struggled with language barriers and customer support issues. Kofo was determined to remove those obstacles.

The AI-Powered Transformation: Automating Sellapy's Growth

Kofo had always known that innovation was the key to staying ahead, especially when competing in a global marketplace. After the third iteration of Sellapy began gaining traction, Kofo faced a new challenge: how could he scale customer engagement and streamline operations without the budget for a full-fledged marketing team? He knew that without the right tools, even a good idea could plateau, leaving potential untapped.

This time, the answer was clear: **Artificial Intelligence (AI)**.

Kofo decided to leverage AI-powered solutions to create the marketing and engagement infrastructure that Sellapy desperately needed. Instead of hiring a large marketing team, he opted for a cutting-edge AI system that would act as his invisible workforce, doing everything from customer engagement to process automation. The result wasn't just operational efficiency—it was a transformation in how Sellapy interacted with its vendors and customers.

Lead Funnel Management

First, Kofo implemented an AI-powered lead funnel management system to streamline how potential vendors and customers interacted with the platform. The system tracked users' journeys from their first visit to the site all the way through sign-up and purchase, sending personalized emails and text messages at each stage to keep them engaged. By automating this process, Sellapy could follow up with interested users, send tailored offers, and guide vendors through the onboarding process, all without human intervention.

Customer Reviews and Messaging

Next, Kofo knew that trust was essential for a global marketplace. To help vendors build credibility, the AI system automatically requested customer reviews after each transaction, improving engagement and ensuring vendors received valuable feedback. This not only boosted confidence for new buyers but also created a sense of transparency, where customers could see the experiences of others before making a purchase.

The messaging system was another crucial upgrade. Missed opportunities due to unanswered inquiries had been a problem for vendors, especially those operating in different time zones. Kofo solved this by introducing AI messaging bots capable of responding to customer queries in real time, 24/7. These bots weren't just generic responders—they were designed to learn from previous interactions, offering increasingly personalized responses as they gained more data.

Emailing and Missed Call Text Back
With the influx of new users, Kofo also needed a more effective email marketing strategy. The AI-powered email automation took care of sending personalized newsletters, promotional offers, and updates to both vendors and buyers. The system used behavioural insights to tailor messages based on customer preferences, ensuring higher open and click-through rates.

One of Kofo's most ingenious implementations was the missed call text-back feature. When a vendor or customer tried to reach Sellapy's support team but couldn't get through, the AI system would automatically send a text message, acknowledging the missed call and offering alternative ways to resolve the issue—whether through chat, email, or scheduling a call back. These kept customers engaged and showed that Sellapy was always on hand, even when live support wasn't available.

AI Agents: Personalising the Experience

Kofo wanted Sellapy to feel like more than just a transaction platform, it needed to feel like a personal shopping experience, even at scale. For this, he implemented AI-powered shopping agents that acted like personal assistants for buyers. These agents helped users find products based on their preferences, previous purchases, and browsing habits. The AI algorithms made product recommendations in real time, ensuring that each customer felt like the platform understood their needs.

For vendors, these AI agents provided customer service automation, handling everything from answering basic product inquiries to managing returns and processing refunds. The vendors, many of whom lacked the resources to offer 24/7 customer support, now had an always-available team that ensured they could meet customer needs around the clock.

Social Media Content Creation and Posting

As a bootstrapped startup, Kofo knew the value of social media but didn't have the resources to manage it manually. Enter AI once again. Kofo used an AI-driven content creation and social media posting system that automatically generated product highlights, promotional posts, and behind-the-scenes updates for Sellapy's social media channels. The AI system even analysed trends and user engagement to optimize post timing, hashtags, and visuals, ensuring that Sellapy's presence on platforms like Instagram, Facebook, and LinkedIn remained active and appealing without the need for a dedicated team.

Fraud Detection

In the world of global eCommerce, fraud can cripple a platform's reputation. Kofo integrated AI-based fraud detection systems that continuously monitored transactions for any suspicious activity. These systems analysed buying patterns, flagged unusual behaviour, and even learned from past fraudulent attempts, adapting their algorithms to become more effective over time. This helped maintain the integrity of the platform, assuring both vendors and customers that they were operating in a secure environment.

The Result: AI as Sellapy's Secret Weapon

By using AI-powered solutions, Kofo turned Sellapy into a streamlined, automated machine that could handle marketing, customer service, fraud detection, and personalized shopping experiences without the overhead costs of large teams. The AI systems didn't just fill the gaps—they became the backbone of Sellapy's operations, helping Kofo deliver a world-class experience on a global scale.

Instead of being overwhelmed by the challenges of scaling a global marketplace, Kofo harnessed the power of AI to grow Sellapy efficiently, improving customer engagement, enhancing vendor support, and solidifying the platform's reputation as a reliable, ethical marketplace for SMEs everywhere.

Kofo's decision to use AI as his marketing and operational team wasn't just a cost-saving measure—it was a strategic innovation that allowed Sellapy to scale faster, serve customers better, and stay ahead of the competition.

Sellapy became more than a marketplace—it became a **gateway to the world** for these small enterprises. Kofo's vision was simple: **"Empowering Global Trade for Every Vendor, Everywhere."** Through seamless **cross-border payments**, reliable logistics partnerships, and **localised support** in multiple languages, Sellapy gave vendors the tools to **sell internationally with confidence**.

But this was more than just a business—it was about **creating a platform rooted in ethics and sustainability**. Kofo didn't just want to build a marketplace; he wanted to build a community where responsible commerce could thrive. Sellapy promoted ethical business practices, ensuring that buyers could trust the vendors they interacted with. From eco-friendly products to fair trade items, the platform allowed buyers to discover **unique products from diverse cultures**, knowing they were contributing to something meaningful.

Kofo's journey with Sellapy had come full circle. What started as a small idea for a local marketplace had grown into a **global platform that empowered SMEs** around the world. And the key to its success wasn't just in the technology it was in **Kofo's relentless focus on solving real problems for real people**.

He had learned that failure wasn't something to be feared; it was a **necessary ingredient** for innovation. Each pivot, each setback, had taught him how to better serve his customers and refine his vision. And in the end, Sellapy became the marketplace it was always meant to be **a platform where every vendor, regardless of size or location, could thrive on the global stage**.

Remarkably, Kofo decided to pivot Sellapy into a more comprehensive platform, not just for eco-friendly products but for **SMEs globally**. He recognized that small businesses needed a platform where they could **buy and sell** locally and globally without the complexities and high costs associated with larger eCommerce giants. He implemented artificial intelligence (AI) tools from **SellapyTech** to help automate parts of the selling process, making it easier for vendors to manage their storefronts.

Slowly but surely, Sellapy began to gain traction. Kofo had built a platform that solved real problems for small businesses, and the lessons from his past failures guided his decisions. He didn't just rebuild Sellapy—he reinvented it based on the lessons of the past, using each setback as fuel for greater innovation.

Actionable Takeaways

Here are three ways you can use failure as a tool for innovation in your own journey:

1. **Extract the Lessons**: After every failure, ask yourself, "What went wrong, and why?" Focus on extracting actionable lessons from the experience rather than seeing the failure as a reflection of your abilities. Use those lessons to refine your strategy moving forward.

2. **Pivot with Data, Not Emotion**: If you're thinking about pivoting your business or idea, make sure it's based on concrete data—market trends, customer feedback, and user behaviour. Pivot with purpose, and use the insights you've gained from previous setbacks to guide your next move.

3. **Embrace Constraints**: When resources are limited, view those constraints as an opportunity to innovate. Kofo's lack of funding pushed him to develop creative, low-cost marketing strategies. Sometimes, the absence of resources can spark your most innovative solutions.

Kofo's journey with Sellapy demonstrates that **failure isn't final**, it's part of the process. By embracing failure as an opportunity for growth and innovation, you can build something even stronger than what you started with. **Setbacks are simply setups for your next breakthrough.**

"When you learn to see failure as a signal to adapt, you turn obstacles into opportunities for reinvention."

In the next chapter, we'll explore how Kofo **led with purpose**, aligning his vision with a deeper mission to create impact both locally and globally.

Chapter 4

Leading with Purpose

Part 1: Kofo's Leadership Transformation

As Sellapy continued to grow, Kofo realized that his role was shifting from just being an entrepreneur to becoming a **leader** with a clear sense of purpose. The early days of **survival mode**—where every decision was about staying afloat—had given way to bigger questions: What kind of company did he want to build? What kind of leader did he want to be? And, more importantly, what **impact** did he want Sellapy to have beyond just making profits?

One defining moment came during a meeting with his core team. Sellapy had successfully started to carve out a niche as a global marketplace for SMEs, but Kofo noticed something troubling. While they had scaled operationally, there was a sense of **disconnect** between his team and the company's larger vision. His employees were going through the motions—handling tasks, meeting targets—but Kofo could tell that they were losing sight of the **"why"** behind their work. For Kofo, that was a problem.

He hadn't built Sellapy just to become another faceless eCommerce platform. From the very beginning, his goal was to **empower small businesses** and promote ethical commerce on a global scale. He wanted Sellapy to represent more than just a profit-driven company—it had to stand for something bigger. But the rapid growth and day-to-day operations had caused that larger vision to blur, even for him.

In that meeting, as Kofo sat at the head of the table, he decided to **reset the tone** of Sellapy's leadership and mission. It was no longer enough to just grow; they needed to grow **with purpose**. He stood up and addressed his team with a renewed sense of clarity.

"Sellapy exists for a reason," he began, looking around the room. "We're not here to just make money or be another online marketplace. Our mission is to **empower people**—business owners who don't have the resources or opportunities to sell globally, and consumers who want to buy responsibly. Every single thing we do needs to reflect that mission. I need each of you to feel that purpose, to lead with it, and to make it part of your everyday work."

That moment marked the start of Kofo's transformation as a leader. He understood that if Sellapy was going to thrive in the long term, it had to be driven by a **purpose that went beyond profits**—a purpose that resonated not just with customers, but with his employees, stakeholders, and the broader community.

Principle: How Purpose-Driven Leadership Creates Sustainable Success

Kofo's story reveals a powerful lesson for every entrepreneur and leader: **Purpose-driven leadership** is the cornerstone of **lasting success**. When you lead with purpose, you don't just inspire your team—you give them a reason to go above and beyond, to feel invested in the company's mission, and to align their personal values with the work they do. A business without purpose can generate revenue, but it won't create lasting impact or loyalty.

Here's why leading with purpose is so critical to long-term success:

1. **Purpose Builds Resilience**: When your team understands the deeper reason behind their work, they're more likely to push through difficult times. For Kofo, the challenges of scaling Sellapy—from

technical failures to funding issues—were easier to navigate because he had a clear sense of purpose. His commitment to empowering SMEs wasn't just a business strategy; it was the **foundation of the company**. Purpose gives people something to hold onto when times get tough, making them more resilient in the face of adversity.

2. **Purpose Drives Innovation**: Kofo's commitment to ethical commerce and empowering small businesses didn't just guide his leadership style—it also drove innovation at Sellapy. For example, when he decided to integrate AI-powered solutions into the platform, it wasn't just about efficiency; it was about finding creative ways to help vendors succeed. When your leadership is driven by purpose, you'll consistently seek out new ways to serve your mission, which in turn drives innovation. Purpose becomes the guiding force behind every decision.

3. **Purpose Attracts and Retains Talent**: In today's world, employees are no longer satisfied with just a paycheck. They want to work for companies that align with their personal values and are making a positive impact in the world. By

leading with purpose, Kofo was able to **attract top talent** who believed in Sellapy's mission. His team wasn't just working for a paycheck, they were working to empower small businesses, promote sustainability, and create lasting change. This sense of purpose led to higher employee satisfaction, lower turnover, and a more engaged workforce.

4. **Purpose Builds Trust with Customers**: Consumers today are increasingly looking to spend their money with companies that reflect their values. Kofo's focus on promoting ethical commerce and empowering SMEs wasn't just a feel-good mission—it became one of Sellapy's greatest competitive advantages. Buyers trusted the platform because they knew they were supporting businesses that aligned with their values. Leading with purpose helped Kofo build **brand loyalty**, making customers feel good about choosing Sellapy over other global marketplaces.

"Leadership is not about driving results; it's about inspiring people to see the purpose behind the results."

Part 2: Leading the Team with Purpose

After that pivotal meeting, Kofo began leading Sellapy with a renewed sense of clarity. He started holding **purpose-driven workshops** with his team, where they reconnected with the company's mission and values. He encouraged every employee, from the customer service agents to the tech developers, to think about how their work contributed to the larger goal of **empowering global trade for small businesses**.

He also began implementing **transparent leadership practices**, where he regularly communicated the company's mission, goals, and challenges. Rather than shielding his team from the realities of running a global business, he opened up the conversation, allowing them to contribute ideas and solutions. This kind of leadership, one that fosters openness and collaboration—allowed Sellapy to navigate complex problems with a unified sense of purpose.

One of the most significant shifts came when Kofo empowered his team to take **ownership** of the company's mission. He encouraged them to think like leaders in their respective roles, asking themselves how they could push Sellapy's mission forward. Whether it was a developer creating a new feature or a marketing specialist crafting campaign, each person had a **clear understanding of the purpose behind their work**.

As Sellapy continued to expand, it wasn't just a marketplace anymore, it had become a **movement**. Vendors around the world felt connected to something bigger than a platform; they felt part of a community that supported ethical trade, responsible commerce, and global connection.

Kofo had learned the most valuable lesson of leadership: when you lead with purpose, you don't just grow a business—you create a lasting legacy.

"When you lead with purpose, you don't just create a business—you ignite a movement that others want to be part of."

Part 3: The Power of Partnership - Building Sellapy with Sunshine

In the midst of Sellapy's growth, Kofo wasn't building the business alone. Behind every bold decision, every sleepless night, and every major pivot was the steady, unwavering support of his partner and lover, **Sunshine**, whom Kofo affectionately called his **"inestimable sweetie pie"**. Sunshine wasn't just a partner in his personal life; she was the **first active vendor** on the new iteration of Sellapy and, more importantly, the foundation of his emotional and strategic support system.

Sunshine had been with Kofo from the very beginning, back when Sellapy was still just an idea scribbled in a notebook. She had believed in his vision long before the platform had any users, funding, or traction. And when Sellapy finally launched its third iteration—targeting small and medium-sized enterprises (SMEs) and vendors looking to go global—it was **Sunshine** who took the bold step of becoming the first vendor on the platform.

She didn't just list her products; she brought her community with her. Sunshine had a strong network of artisans and small business owners who trusted her, and through her influence, she onboarded **thousands of new vendors** to Sellapy, turning what could have been a slow start into a booming marketplace within weeks. But Sunshine's role went far beyond vendor engagement.

Building Together: A Partnership Rooted in Trust
Sunshine had always been a **quiet force of encouragement** in Kofo's life, but as Sellapy evolved, she became something even more vital—a **true business partner**. While Kofo handled the technical side of the platform, Sunshine took charge of vendor onboarding, ensuring that new sellers were properly supported and understood how to leverage the global marketplace. She hosted workshops, wrote vendor guides, and even set up webinars to teach small business owners how to use the platform efficiently. Sunshine wasn't just helping Kofo—she was actively building the Sellapy ecosystem alongside him.

And when it came to funding, Sunshine once again stepped up. During a critical period when Sellapy was struggling to raise capital, it was Sunshine who injected her personal savings into the business. She believed in Kofo's dream so deeply that she was willing to take the financial risk, ensuring that Sellapy had the runway it needed to scale. This wasn't just an act of love—it was an act of **partnership**, where the lines between business and personal were blurred in the best possible way.

"This is our dream," Sunshine would often tell Kofo during late-night strategy sessions. **"And we're going to build it together."**

Brainstorming the 'Leading with Purpose' Moment

One of the most pivotal moments in Kofo's leadership journey—when he realised that Sellapy needed to refocus on its purpose—was a direct result of his long conversations with Sunshine. As Sellapy grew, Kofo found himself getting lost in the day-to-day operations. There were technical issues to solve, vendors to onboard, and marketing strategies to refine. He was working harder than ever, but he couldn't shake the feeling that the company's **soul** was slipping away. It was Sunshine who helped him refocus.

One evening, after a particularly gruelling day, Sunshine sat Kofo down with a cup of tea. They began to talk, not about the technical aspects of Sellapy, but about its **purpose**. Sunshine reminded him of why he had started the platform in the first place, to **empower small businesses** and create a **global community of responsible commerce**. They brainstormed together, exploring how they could realign Sellapy's operations with its core mission. Sunshine's insights were invaluable; she had always had a **keen understanding** of people and their motivations.

"It's not just about making Sellapy bigger," she said. **"It's about making it better, about reminding ourselves and everyone else why we're doing this in the first place."**

That conversation was the catalyst for Kofo's **purpose-driven leadership reset**, where he called his team together and refocused the company's mission. Sunshine's ability to see the bigger picture, combined with her deep emotional intelligence, was what helped Kofo shift from a purely operational leader to a visionary one.

The Invaluable Role of a Supportive Partner

As Sellapy continued to grow, Kofo often reflected on how different his journey would have been without Sunshine. She wasn't just a sounding board or a passive observer, she was **actively shaping the business** alongside him. Sunshine's presence made leadership feel possible, even during the most challenging times.

Kofo knew that being a **successful leader** in both business and life required having the right people beside you. Sunshine embodied everything he needed in a partner, someone who believed in his vision, contributed her own ideas, and supported him emotionally and financially. Her faith in Sellapy's mission and in Kofo himself allowed him to push through the hardest moments with renewed confidence.

The truth Kofo came to understand was simple: **leading with purpose becomes infinitely more achievable when you have a partner who shares that purpose with you**. Sunshine didn't just support Kofo; she was his **co-architect**, building Sellapy brick by brick, side by side with him. She challenged him when he needed it, comforted him when he doubted himself, and celebrated every win as if it were her own.

Principle: Success is Stronger with a Supportive Partner

Kofo's journey with Sunshine illustrates a critical lesson for leaders and entrepreneurs alike: **success is rarely a solo endeavour**. The presence of a **supportive partner**, whether in business or in life, can elevate your leadership, push you through adversity, and help you realize your full potential. Here's why:

1. **Shared Vision, Shared Strength**

   When you have a partner who believes in your vision as much as you do, the journey becomes less daunting. Sunshine wasn't just along for the ride; she shared Kofo's vision for Sellapy and contributed to it actively. This **shared sense of purpose** made them both stronger and more resilient.

2. **Emotional and Financial Support**

   Building a business comes with emotional and financial pressures, and without the right support system, it's easy to burn out. Sunshine provided Kofo with both emotional encouragement and financial backing when Sellapy needed it most. Her investment in the company was a reflection of her investment in their shared future.

3. **Collaborative Leadership**

   Kofo's leadership wasn't shaped in isolation. Sunshine's insights and perspectives helped him grow as a leader, guiding his decisions during key moments of the company's evolution. Having someone to brainstorm with, who challenges you to think deeper, is invaluable for any leader.

Actionable Takeaways

1. **Involve Your Partner in the Vision**: Whether they are actively involved in the business or simply supporting you from the side-lines, ensure your partner understands and believes in your vision. When you share the journey, you amplify your strength.
2. **Embrace Collaborative Leadership**: Don't be afraid to lean on your partner for insights, ideas, or advice. Their perspective can offer you clarity in moments when you might be too close to the situation to see it clearly.

3. **Celebrate Wins Together**: Success is sweeter when you celebrate it with the people who helped you achieve it. Whether it's a small victory or a major milestone, make time to acknowledge and appreciate your partner's contributions.

Kofo's story, intertwined with Sunshine's support, demonstrates the **inestimable power of partnership**. Their journey together not only shaped Sellapy into the global marketplace it became but also redefined Kofo's approach to leadership. In the next chapter, we'll explore how Kofo and Sunshine navigated **strategic risk-taking** as they made bold decisions that propelled Sellapy to new heights, with Sunshine by his side every step of the way.

"Behind every great leader is a partner who strengthens their purpose, shares their vision, and walks beside them in every step of the journey."

This chapter underscores the immense role a **supportive partner** plays in both personal and professional success, making Kofo and Sunshine's teamwork a core part of Sellapy's growth.

Chapter 5

Strategic Risk-Taking for Growth

Part 1: The Bold Move That Changed Everything

It was just after midnight when Kofo sat at his desk, staring at the numbers on his screen. The reports were clear: **Sellapy** was growing, but not fast enough. The platform had built a loyal customer base, vendors were onboarding daily, and the global marketplace was finally starting to see the traction Kofo had worked so hard for. But there was still one glaring problem: Sellapy wasn't scaling at the speed necessary to compete with the bigger eCommerce giants.

Kofo knew that Sellapy needed to expand, and fast. The marketplace model they had built was working, but if they didn't **take bold steps to scale**, they risked stagnation. However, scaling wasn't going to be easy. It required significant investment in marketing, infrastructure, and technology. This was a **make-or-break moment**.

"We have to take a risk," Kofo thought, but he wasn't alone in this decision.

Sunshine was in the next room, and she had been right there with him through every challenge, pivot, and success. They had worked as a team from the beginning, and this moment was no different. Kofo walked into the living room, where Sunshine was reviewing some vendor feedback from the latest onboarding session. He sat next to her, the weight of the decision heavy on his mind.

"We need to scale Sellapy," Kofo said, breaking the silence. **"I'm thinking about a massive push, investing heavily in AI, expanding our marketing, and going global in a bigger way. But it's risky. If it doesn't work, we could lose everything we've built."**

Sunshine looked up from her notes, her face calm and thoughtful. She had always been the **rational voice** in their partnership, balancing Kofo's bold ideas with careful consideration. But this time, something was different.

"Kofo, we've come this far because we took risks," she said, leaning in. **"Calculated risks, yes, but bold ones. This isn't the time to play it safe. If we want Sellapy to be the global marketplace we've always envisioned, we have to take this step. Together."**

Her words hung in the air, solidifying what Kofo had already known deep down. He trusted Sunshine implicitly—her instincts, her support, and her ability to see the bigger picture. With her by his side, he felt more confident that this was the right move.

They spent the next few hours hashing out the details: how they would fund the expansion, where they would allocate resources, and what the **potential risks and rewards** could be. Sunshine, ever practical, suggested they bring in a small advisory board, people they trusted who had experience with scaling businesses globally. Kofo agreed, knowing that surrounding themselves with the right expertise would mitigate some of the risk.

Principle: The Importance of Calculated Risks

Kofo and Sunshine's decision to take a bold step toward scaling Sellapy was a pivotal moment in their journey. It wasn't reckless, **it was calculated**. They knew that without taking risks, there would be no growth. But they also understood that **not all risks are equal**, and knowing how to evaluate, measure, and take calculated risks was the key to their success.

Here's why **strategic risk-taking** is essential for growth:

1. **Stagnation is a Bigger Risk**

   One of the most common mistakes businesses make is playing it too safe. Kofo knew that if Sellapy continued on its current trajectory without taking any major leaps, it risked becoming stagnant. In today's competitive global market, standing still is just as dangerous as moving backward. By recognizing the risk of **stagnation**, Kofo and Sunshine were able to make a proactive decision to scale.

2. **Risk Assessment Tools**

   Before taking any major leap, Kofo and Sunshine always ran their ideas through a **risk assessment process**. They evaluated potential downsides and asked themselves two crucial questions: **What's**

the worst-case scenario, and can we survive it? If the answer was yes, they moved forward with confidence. This approach allowed them to take bold steps while still protecting Sellapy's core business.

3. **Surround Yourself with Expertise**

   Kofo and Sunshine understood the importance of surrounding themselves with the right advisors. Bringing in a small advisory board of trusted experts allowed them to gain valuable insight into the global marketplace, minimizing risk by learning from others who had already walked the path of scaling a business. When taking strategic risks, you don't have to go it alone, leveraging expertise can be the difference between success and failure.

4. **Bet on Innovation**

   Part of Kofo's bold strategy was to **invest heavily in AI and technology**. This was a risk because it required significant upfront investment, but Kofo and Sunshine knew that **innovation was the future**. They had already seen the power of AI in transforming Sellapy's operations, and they believed that doubling down on this technology would allow them to outpace competitors and offer something unique in the global marketplace. Sometimes, the best risks are the ones that involve betting on future trends.

"The greatest risk isn't in the bold leap you take—it's in the opportunity you miss by standing still."

Part 2: The Leap That Paid Off

Kofo and Sunshine made the decision to go all-in. They restructured Sellapy's budget, pouring funds into a **global marketing campaign**, expanding their AI infrastructure, and enhancing the platform's capacity to handle **massive user growth**. They partnered with influencers in key markets, launched targeted digital ads, and pushed Sellapy into markets they had never entered before.

At first, the results were slow. The investments were heavy, and the pressure mounted. Kofo and Sunshine found themselves working long hours, constantly checking numbers, adjusting strategies, and fine-tuning their approach. But they never wavered in their belief that this risk was necessary.

Then, just as they had hoped, the breakthrough came.

Sellapy's vendor onboarding skyrocketed, with thousands of new businesses signing up from countries all over the world. Buyers were flocking to the platform, excited by the global, ethical marketplace that Kofo and Sunshine had built. The **AI-powered infrastructure** they had invested in allowed Sellapy to handle the flood of new users seamlessly, without crashes or delays. The risk had paid off.

Sellapy wasn't just growing, it was scaling globally, and Kofo and Sunshine's bold decision to take that leap was the reason.

Kofo and Sunshine's willingness to take **strategic, calculated risks** is what ultimately pushed Sellapy from a promising startup to a **global marketplace powerhouse**. Their story is a testament to the fact that without bold moves, there can be no bold success. In the next chapter, we'll dive deeper into how they mastered **influence and persuasion**, building partnerships that would propel Sellapy into the international spotlight.

"Calculated risks turn dreams into reality when you have the courage to leap and the wisdom to measure the fall."

Part 3: The Bold Gamble That Paid Off, The Birth of SellapyTech

The air in the office was thick with anticipation as Kofo and Sunshine sat quietly, watching the numbers refresh on their dashboard. It had been months since they had decided to take the biggest risk of their entrepreneurial journey—doubling down on **AI infrastructure**, betting heavily on a global marketing campaign, and most daring of all, **using other people's money** to scale **Sellapy**. They had leveraged **business credit** to fund the expansion, a move that had made their financial advisor uncomfortable.

But Kofo and Sunshine weren't after comfort, they were after **scale**. The dream was bigger than the fear of debt, and now they waited to see if the gamble would pay off.

It hadn't been an easy decision. The weight of using business credit hung over them like a dark cloud, especially since they had always prided themselves on being a

bootstrapped operation. This time, though, the stakes were too high. They needed the financial power to push **Sellapy** into the global eCommerce space, where giants ruled and competition was fierce. The decision to scale meant they had to act fast, and personal savings alone wouldn't cut it.

Leveraging **other people's money**, whether through business credit lines or external investors was a calculated risk. If Sellapy didn't take off as planned, the debt would come crashing down on them. Worse, it could mean losing everything they had built so far. But Sunshine, ever the clear thinker, had reminded Kofo of their previous conversations.

"**The greatest risk is not moving forward,**" she had said one evening as they went over the financials. "**We have the data; we know our marketplace works. Now it's time to fuel it.**"

So, they took the leap. They invested heavily in **AI-driven automation**, expanding Sellapy's infrastructure to handle more vendors, automate processes, and personalize shopping experiences for millions of users around the globe. The risk wasn't just in the technology, it was in the **financial structure** they had set up to fuel the expansion.

The Skyrocket: AI Infrastructure and Scaling Sellapy

The AI infrastructure Kofo and Sunshine implemented was designed to do more than just support growth, it was built to **transform the marketplace into a truly global powerhouse**. As vendors flooded onto the platform, Sellapy's AI-powered systems handled everything from **lead funnel management** to **real-time product recommendations**.

With AI in place, Sellapy could automatically onboard thousands of new vendors, managing listings, product descriptions, and even pricing suggestions based on market trends. AI bots were also integrated into **customer service**, handling inquiries around the clock, ensuring buyers always had answers, even when human staff were unavailable.

But the most transformative part of the AI infrastructure was its ability to **personalize the customer experience**. By analysing buyer behaviour, purchase history, and even browsing patterns, the AI system could recommend products with uncanny precision. Customers began spending more time on the platform, and average order values skyrocketed as buyers discovered new products that aligned perfectly with their preferences. **Sellapy wasn't just a marketplace anymore, it was an intelligent ecosystem** that knew how to make every customer feel like the platform was built just for them.

The results were **astonishing**. Vendor sign-ups surged, customer engagement hit an all-time high, and revenue shot through the roof. In just a few months, Sellapy had grown beyond what Kofo had ever imagined. The AI infrastructure worked flawlessly, scaling the platform without breaking a sweat.

But the true **masterstroke** came when Kofo realized that their proprietary AI infrastructure wasn't just useful for Sellapy—it could be a standalone product. Businesses around the world were struggling with automation, customer engagement, and AI integration, and Kofo and Sunshine were sitting on the very solution they needed.

It was time to **birth a new company**.

The Birth of SellapyTech: Monetizing the AI Revolution

Sellapy's success was undeniable, but Kofo's entrepreneurial instincts told him there was more to this story. The AI infrastructure they had built for Sellapy wasn't just a tool, it was an entire **business model** waiting to be unleashed. The more he thought about it, the more it made sense: they had perfected the art of **AI-driven eCommerce solutions**, and now they could package it and sell it to other companies.

That's when the idea for **SellapyTech** was born.

SellapyTech became the **subsidiary** that offered AI-driven solutions to other businesses, helping them automate customer service, optimize lead funnels, personalize user experiences, and integrate fraud detection systems—all the tools that had made Sellapy successful. It was a risk to launch a new company while Sellapy was still scaling, but Kofo and Sunshine knew they had the **expertise and the technology** to make it work.

They had already taken the plunge into **using business credit** and other people's money to scale Sellapy, and now, they decided to funnel part of those funds into launching SellapyTech. It was another gamble, but this time, the stakes were even higher. They were betting on their own **AI technology** to be valuable enough that other companies would pay millions for it.

The initial launch of SellapyTech was slow. They faced competition from larger tech firms with more established reputations, but Kofo's and Sunshine's **real-world success** with Sellapy gave them a competitive edge. They had a **proven model**, and more importantly, they had the trust of vendors and clients who had seen first hand how the AI infrastructure worked.

Within a year, SellapyTech had taken off. They signed contracts with major eCommerce companies, offering **custom AI solutions** that allowed businesses to automate their processes, manage customer service with AI agents, and create **personalised shopping experiences**. The AI systems also included **fraud detection**, which was a huge selling point for companies looking to protect their platforms from fraudulent activity.

The risk they had taken, the one that had kept them up at night, worrying about debt and failure had paid off beyond their wildest dreams. **SellapyTech** wasn't just a subsidiary, it had become a **multi-million-pound business** in its own right. The AI technology they had developed for Sellapy was now **revolutionizing other companies**, and the revenue streams were consistent and growing.

The Financial Gamble: Business Credit and Other People's Money

Looking back, the decision to use **business credit** and other people's money was a defining moment in Kofo's and Sunshine's entrepreneurial journey. The risk of debt had loomed large, but they had **trusted the process**. They had built a business model that they believed in, and they were willing to bet on themselves.

They had used **strategic debt** to scale Sellapy, knowing that without the financial power to fuel growth, they would remain stagnant. It wasn't easy there were sleepless nights, high-stakes meetings, and moments of doubt. But in the end, the risk wasn't just necessary, it was the reason for their success.

Sellapy had become a global marketplace with **millions of users**, and **SellapyTech** was now generating consistent **multi-million-pound revenues** by helping other companies replicate the same success. The leap they had taken, trusting AI technology, leveraging credit, and investing in the future had turned their vision into reality.

Actionable Takeaways

1. **Evaluate the Risk of Staying Still**

   Before dismissing bold moves as "too risky," ask yourself what the cost of **not taking the risk** could be. Will staying on your current path lead to stagnation? Sometimes, the greatest risk is **doing nothing**.

2. **Use a Risk Assessment Framework**

   Develop a simple framework for evaluating potential risks. Ask yourself: What's the worst that could happen? Can you survive it? What's the potential upside? Having a clear framework helps take the emotion out of the decision and allows you to assess risk logically.

3. **Leverage Strategic Debt Wisely**

   Using business credit or other people's money isn't always a bad thing if you have a clear strategy. Kofo and Sunshine didn't take on debt recklessly, they used it to scale their business and invest in innovation. When used wisely, debt can be a powerful tool for growth.

4. **Monetize Your Infrastructure**

    The AI infrastructure that powered Sellapy became the foundation for a new, highly profitable business; SellapyTech. If you've developed a unique tool or system that works for your business, consider whether it could become a product or service you can sell to others.

5. **Bet on Future Innovation**

    Kofo and Sunshine's biggest gamble was their investment in AI technology. They bet on future innovation, knowing that **AI** would be a critical part of the eCommerce landscape. Investing in the future is always a risk, but it's often the key to staying ahead of the competition.

Kofo and Sunshine's story isn't just one of bold risks, it's a testament to the power of **strategic decision-making**, **innovation**, and **trusting in the long-term vision**. The AI infrastructure that transformed Sellapy into a global powerhouse didn't just solve their immediate business problems, it gave birth to **SellapyTech**, a company that continues to make millions in revenue by helping others achieve the same kind of success.

This section highlights the strategic risks that Kofo and Sunshine took with **AI infrastructure** and **business credit**, leading to massive success and the birth of **SellapyTech**.

"Big risks bring big rewards when you trust your vision, invest in the future, and aren't afraid to bet on yourself."

In the next chapter, we'll explore how Kofo and Sunshine mastered **influence and persuasion**, forging key partnerships that elevated Sellapy even further, pushing their success to new heights.

Chapter 6

The Art of Influence and Persuasion

Part 1: The Deal That Changed Everything

It was a quiet afternoon in London, but the meeting room at Sellapy's office was anything but calm. The tension was thick as Kofo and Sunshine sat across from one of the largest international logistics companies in the world. It was a pivotal meeting one that could either propel **Sellapy** into a new era of growth or force them to rethink their global strategy.

Kofo and Sunshine had built Sellapy into a flourishing marketplace, but the platform's biggest challenge was the high cost and complexity of international shipping. Without reliable, affordable logistics partners, they couldn't offer their vendors the global reach they had promised. The solution? Securing a deal with a logistics giant that would allow them to scale internationally with reduced costs.

The only problem was that Sellapy was still relatively small compared to their competitors, and Kofo knew the logistics company wouldn't offer a favourable deal unless they believed in Sellapy's vision. They weren't just selling a product, they were selling a **dream** of empowering small businesses worldwide through eCommerce.

As the meeting started, the company's executives began with their usual talking points, cost structures, delivery windows, and contract terms. They laid out their conditions, most of which would strain Sellapy's margins. The numbers weren't in their favour, but Kofo and Sunshine weren't there to talk numbers alone. They were there to use their **influence and persuasion** to create a deal that would benefit both sides.

Sunshine started speaking, her voice calm but powerful. She didn't focus on the costs or the logistics right away; instead, she painted a picture of the future they could build together. **"We're not just asking for a shipping deal,"** she said, looking each executive in the eye. **"We're asking you to be a part of something bigger. We're connecting thousands of small businesses to the**

global marketplace. We're building a future where local artisans, entrepreneurs, and vendors can access customers across the world, and we want you to be the logistics backbone of that movement."

Her words hung in the air, and Kofo could see the shift in the room. The executives were no longer thinking about costs and risks; they were thinking about the **potential** to be a part of something that could change the landscape of eCommerce. Sunshine wasn't just selling a service, she was selling an idea, a vision of what they could create together.

Kofo then stepped in with the specifics. He laid out the benefits for the logistics company, how working with Sellapy would allow them to access untapped markets, how they could leverage Sellapy's growing vendor base to generate new revenue streams, and how their partnership could transform the way small businesses operated on a global scale.

By the end of the meeting, the logistics company was no longer focused on squeezing Sellapy for margins. They had been persuaded by something far more compelling: the

possibility of making history as the logistics partner of a global eCommerce revolution.

Principle: How to Use Influence and Persuasion to Create Strategic Partnerships

Kofo and Sunshine's ability to secure a deal with one of the largest logistics companies in the world was not about offering the best numbers. It was about leveraging their **influence** and using **strategic persuasion** to show their partners the **bigger picture**. They understood that the most successful deals aren't made by arguing over details—they're made by appealing to people's desire to be part of something meaningful.

Here's how they used influence and persuasion to win big:

1. **Sell the Vision, Not Just the Product**: People are more likely to support a business when they believe in its **mission**. Kofo and Sunshine didn't just talk about shipping and logistics—they painted a picture of the **impact** their partnership could have on the world. This shifted the conversation from costs to **value**. When you're trying to influence someone, don't just sell the product—sell the vision of what you can create together.

2. **Understand the Other Party's Motivations**: Before going into the meeting, Kofo and Sunshine had done their homework. They knew that the logistics company was looking to expand into emerging markets and wanted to increase its foothold in the eCommerce space. By showing how partnering with Sellapy would help them achieve their goals, they tapped into the company's **existing desires**. To persuade effectively, you need to understand what the other side wants and frame your offer as the solution to their needs.

3. **Create a Win-Win Scenario**: One of the keys to successful persuasion is creating a **win-win situation**. Kofo and Sunshine didn't just present their case as something that would benefit Sellapy, they showed how the logistics company would win as well. They emphasized how the partnership would open new revenue streams for the logistics company and help them gain access to new markets. When both sides see the value in a deal, they are far more likely to come to an agreement.

4. **Use Emotional Appeal**: While numbers and facts are important, **emotional appeal** often seals the deal. Sunshine's words about connecting small

businesses to the global marketplace weren't just facts, they were a **call to action**. She tapped into the emotions of the executives, appealing to their sense of purpose and their desire to be part of something transformative. Persuasion isn't just about logic, it's about making people feel something.

"True influence is not about convincing people to follow you—it's about inspiring them to believe in the future you're creating together."

Part 2: Expanding Influence Beyond One Deal

The success of the logistics partnership was only the beginning. Word quickly spread about **Sellapy's rapid growth**, and soon, Kofo and Sunshine were fielding calls from investors, tech companies, and international partners who wanted to be part of their growing ecosystem. But Kofo knew that influence and persuasion went far beyond just **closing deals**. It was about building **long-term relationships** and establishing a reputation as a trusted leader in the global eCommerce space.

One of the next key partnerships they secured was with a **fintech company** that specialised in cross-border payments. This partnership would allow vendors on Sellapy to **accept payments in multiple currencies**, further enhancing their global reach. But once again, this wasn't just a numbers game, it was about convincing the fintech company that Sellapy was the future of ethical, global commerce.

Kofo and Sunshine used the same tactics that had worked before: they sold the vision, tapped into the company's motivations, and created a win-win scenario. By emphasizing how the partnership would allow the fintech company to expand its footprint in emerging markets, they positioned Sellapy as the perfect platform for their growth. The fintech company signed on, and the partnership brought in millions in new revenue for both sides.

As Sellapy's influence grew, so did the **subsidiary company, SellapyTech**. Kofo and Sunshine used their ability to persuade and influence to secure even more contracts with tech companies looking to integrate **AI-driven solutions** into their own businesses. By this point, Kofo and Sunshine had become known as **master negotiators**, leaders who could **see the bigger picture** and make deals that benefited everyone involved.

Principle: Influence in Leadership and Business

Influence isn't just about **getting what you want**, it's about **inspiring others to believe in your vision** and **creating a network of mutually beneficial relationships**. Here's how you can use influence and persuasion to build strategic partnerships and grow your business:

1. **Build Trust and Credibility**: People are more likely to be influenced by those they trust. Kofo and Sunshine had built a **solid reputation** for

integrity, transparency, and delivering on their promises. To increase your influence, focus on building trust over time through consistent actions and reliability.

2. **Be a Thought Leader**: Kofo and Sunshine positioned themselves as **thought leaders** in the eCommerce and AI space. By sharing their insights and vision through speaking engagements, interviews, and content, they attracted partners who believed in their expertise. Influence grows when others see you as an authority in your field.

3. **Create a Strong Network**: Influence isn't just about individual relationships. It's about building a **network of supporters** who advocate for you. Kofo and Sunshine built strong relationships with their partners, investors, and vendors, which created a **ripple effect** of influence. When others are talking about your business and sharing your vision, your influence expands exponentially.

4. **Focus on Long-Term Relationships**: Kofo and Sunshine weren't just interested in **closing deals**, they were focused on building **long-term partnerships** that would grow with them. They nurtured their relationships, kept in touch with

their partners, and continually found ways to add value. Influence is sustained through long-term commitment, not short-term gains.

Actionable Takeaways

Here are three steps you can take to build influence and use strategic persuasion to grow your business or career:

1. **Sell the Bigger Vision**: Whether you're pitching a product or negotiating a deal, always focus on the **bigger picture**. Show your partners how they can be part of something impactful and transformational, and they'll be more likely to buy in.

2. **Understand the Other Party's Needs**: Before you enter any negotiation, do your homework. Understand what the other side wants and needs, and frame your offer as the solution to their problem. When you make it about **their success**, you increase your influence.

3. **Build Credibility Over Time**: Influence is built through **trust and credibility**. Be consistent in your actions, deliver on your promises, and always act with integrity. The more credible you are, the

more people will trust your vision and be influenced by your ideas.

Kofo and Sunshine's ability to master **influence and persuasion** not only helped them secure key partnerships, it elevated Sellapy and SellapyTech to new levels of success. Their journey shows that the art of influence is not just about **winning deals**, but about **creating lasting relationships** that propel your vision forward.

"Persuasion is not about winning the argument, it's about showing the other side how their success is tied to your vision."

In the next chapter, we'll explore how they **built high-performing teams**, empowering their employees to take ownership of Sellapy's mission and drive the company's success even further.

Chapter 7

Building High-Performing Teams

Part 1: From Founders to Leaders

Kofo stood by the large windows of Sellapy's headquarters, overlooking the bustling streets of London below. The company had grown faster than he could have imagined, but with that growth came a new challenge, one that he and Sunshine had never fully anticipated. They were no longer just the **visionaries** or the hands-on builders of Sellapy. Now, they had to lead something much larger: a diverse and expanding team that needed clear direction and guidance.

It hadn't always been this way. In the early days, Kofo and Sunshine had done everything themselves. They were the **product developers**, the **marketers**, the **customer service agents**, and even the **accountants**. But as Sellapy expanded, they began to hire more employees. People who were skilled, talented, and driven, but who still needed direction. Managing a handful of employees was one thing, but now, Sellapy was **scaling fast**, and the team had grown into multiple departments, each with its own dynamics and challenges.

Kofo realized that if Sellapy was going to reach its full potential, they needed more than just talented individuals. They needed a **high-performing team** that was aligned with their mission and capable of driving the company forward without constant oversight.

But building that kind of team wasn't going to happen overnight.

Sunshine, ever perceptive, had noticed the shifts in team dynamics as well. She had seen how different departments, while effective in their own right, were starting to operate in **silos**. The **spirit of collaboration** that had once been the backbone of their early success was starting to fade. People were focused on their individual tasks, but they weren't always working together toward the larger vision.

One evening, Kofo and Sunshine sat down in their living room, reviewing the feedback from their latest team meeting. **"We've got the right people in the room,"** Kofo said, reflecting on the talent they had gathered. **"But** we need to find a way to bring them together, make them feel like they're part of something bigger."

Sunshine agreed. "**It's not just about having great players**," she said. "It's about building a team that works together. We need to create a culture where everyone feels like they have a stake in Sellapy's success."

Principle: How to Build and Sustain a High-Performing Team

Building a high-performing team is about more than just hiring talented individuals, it's about creating a **culture** of collaboration, ownership, and shared purpose. Here's how Kofo and Sunshine transformed their growing group of employees into a cohesive, high-performing team that drove Sellapy's success.

1. **Create a Shared Vision**: One of the first things Kofo and Sunshine did was to **reconnect the team with Sellapy's mission**. During a company-wide meeting, they didn't just talk about sales targets or product launches. Instead, they

reminded everyone why Sellapy existed: to empower small businesses around the world and create a marketplace that championed ethical commerce. They made sure every department whether in marketing, operations, or customer support—understood how their work contributed to that larger mission.

By doing this, they created a sense of **shared purpose**. Employees were no longer just focused on their individual tasks; they felt like they were part of something bigger, something meaningful. This **alignment** of vision is crucial for any high-performing team.

2. **Foster Collaboration, Not Competition**: As Sellapy's departments grew, Kofo and Sunshine noticed that some teams were starting to **compete** against each other instead of collaborating. This kind of internal competition could be toxic, so they made it a priority to **foster a culture of collaboration**. They introduced **cross-functional projects**, where employees from different departments worked together on key initiatives. These projects encouraged team

members to share knowledge, problem-solve together, and leverage each other's strengths.

One of the most successful initiatives was the **Vendor Experience Project**, where the customer service team worked closely with the technology and marketing teams to improve how vendors onboarded onto the platform. The collaboration not only improved vendor satisfaction but also created a sense of **team unity** across departments.

3. **Empower Through Ownership**: Sunshine was a strong advocate for empowering employees through **ownership**. She believed that when people felt a sense of **ownership** over their work, they were more engaged, motivated, and committed to success. To foster this, they started giving team members the autonomy to make decisions and drive their own projects.

For example, rather than micromanaging every decision, they allowed the marketing team to design their own campaigns and test new strategies. They trusted their team to make the right decisions, and this **trust** created a culture of **innovation**. People felt free to experiment, knowing that they had the support of leadership behind them.

4. **Recognize and Reward Contributions**: One of the key components of building a high-performing team is **recognition**. Kofo and Sunshine understood that if they wanted to keep their team motivated, they needed to recognize and celebrate individual and team achievements regularly. This wasn't just about monetary rewards, it was about acknowledging hard work and effort in front of the entire company.

During company meetings, they made it a point to highlight key wins from each department, whether it was a successful product launch or a new partnership deal. They also implemented a **peer recognition program**, where employees could nominate each other for their contributions. This created a culture where people felt valued, which is essential for maintaining high performance.

"A high-performing team isn't built by individuals working alone—it's built by people who are aligned with a shared vision and work as one."

Part 2: The Turning Point in Team Culture

The true turning point came during one of Sellapy's quarterly leadership meetings. They had just completed the largest vendor onboarding project in the company's history, and the results had exceeded expectations. But it wasn't just the numbers that impressed Kofo and Sunshine—it was the way the team had come together, solving problems as a unit, pushing past obstacles, and supporting each other every step of the way.

During the meeting, Kofo stood up to address the team. **"This is what I'm most proud of,"** he said. **"Not just the growth or the numbers—but the way you all worked together to make it happen. Sellapy is what it is today because of this team, because you took ownership and worked as one."**

The room was quiet for a moment, and then the applause started, slowly at first but then building into a wave of appreciation. It was clear that something had shifted. The employees weren't just workers; they were part of something bigger. They had a stake in Sellapy's future, and they were ready to push it to even greater heights.

From that day on, the **team culture** at Sellapy became one of its greatest strengths. New hires quickly absorbed the collaborative, purpose-driven spirit of the company, and teams across departments worked seamlessly together.

Kofo and Sunshine had learned that the key to scaling a business wasn't just about external growth, it was about **internal alignment**. It was about building a team that was driven by shared values, collaboration, and a collective sense of ownership. That was how Sellapy continued to thrive, long after its early success.

Principle: Sustaining a High-Performing Team

Building a high-performing team is one thing, **sustaining** it is another. Here's how Kofo and Sunshine ensured that Sellapy's team continued to perform at a high level as the company grew:

1. **Continuous Feedback Loops**: Kofo and Sunshine believed in the power of **feedback**, both giving it and receiving it. They encouraged a culture where team members could provide feedback on leadership, processes, and each other. This created a sense of **transparency** and openness, allowing

the team to continuously improve without fear of judgment or retribution.

2. **Adapt and Innovate**: The marketplace was constantly evolving, and so was Sellapy. Kofo and Sunshine made it clear that innovation wasn't just the responsibility of the tech team, it was everyone's job. They encouraged employees to bring new ideas to the table, whether it was for improving internal processes or creating new product features. This **culture of innovation** kept the team agile and forward-thinking, which was critical for sustained high performance.

3. **Prioritize Well-Being and Balance**: High-performing teams can easily burn out if well-being isn't prioritized. Kofo and Sunshine made sure to strike a balance between **hard work and personal well-being**. They introduced flexible work policies, wellness programs, and regular team-building activities. By showing that they cared about their employees' well-being, they created a healthier, more sustainable work environment that fuelled long-term performance.

Actionable Takeaways

Here are three steps you can take to build and sustain a high-performing team in your own business or organization:

1. **Align Your Team with a Shared Mission**: Make sure every employee understands how their work contributes to the larger mission of your company. When people feel like they're part of something meaningful, they're more likely to go above and beyond in their roles.

2. **Empower Ownership and Collaboration**: Give your team members the autonomy to make decisions and take ownership of their work. Foster a culture of collaboration by encouraging cross-functional projects and open communication. High-performing teams are built on trust and mutual respect.

3. **Recognize and Celebrate Wins**: Regularly recognize and celebrate individual and team achievements. Whether it's through public acknowledgment, rewards, or peer recognition programs, showing appreciation goes a long way in motivating your team to keep pushing for excellence.

Kofo and Sunshine's journey in building high-performing teams is a testament to the power of collaboration, empowerment, and shared purpose. Their ability to foster a culture of ownership and innovation is what propelled Sellapy to its greatest successes. In the next chapter, we'll explore how they mastered **time management and balance**, ensuring that as their company scaled, they maintained a healthy balance between growth and personal fulfilment.

> "When ownership and collaboration meet, your team doesn't just perform—they create magic."

As Sellapy continued to scale, Kofo and Sunshine found themselves juggling more than just business growth. They were balancing a rapidly expanding company, a growing team, and their own personal well-being. They realized that **success without balance** could lead to burnout, and that mastering **time management** was crucial not only for their company's longevity but for their own happiness and fulfilment. In the next chapter, we'll explore how Kofo and Sunshine learned to manage their time effectively, ensuring they could grow Sellapy while maintaining a healthy **work-life balance** and achieving **personal fulfilment** along the way.

Chapter 8

Time Mastery and Balance

Part 1: The Breaking Point

It was 3:00 a.m. Kofo sat at his desk, staring at a screen full of unread emails and a never-ending to-do list. The rapid growth of **Sellapy** had brought incredible opportunities, but it had also brought relentless pressure. His days blurred together; meetings, strategy sessions, vendor calls, development sprints, marketing reviews. No matter how much he accomplished, there was always something more waiting for him.

Across the room, Sunshine was typing furiously on her laptop. Like Kofo, she had become engulfed in the demands of running the business. They hadn't had a proper dinner together in weeks, let alone time for themselves. Sellapy was thriving, but Kofo and Sunshine were on the brink of **burnout**.

As Kofo rubbed his temples, exhausted, he began to realize that **something had to change**. Their dedication to the company was unquestionable, but their lives had become consumed by work. They were succeeding in business, but at what cost?

One evening, after yet another marathon work session, Sunshine finally broke the silence. **"Kofo, we can't keep doing this,"** she said, her voice filled with exhaustion. **"We built Sellapy because we believed in empowering small businesses, but we can't sacrifice ourselves in the process. We have to find a way to balance this."**

Kofo nodded, knowing she was right. It wasn't just about the business anymore, it was about their lives. **They needed balance**, or they risked losing the passion that had fuelled Sellapy's success in the first place.

That night, Kofo and Sunshine made a pact. They would no longer allow the company to consume every aspect of their lives. They would learn to **master their time**, delegate more effectively, and carve out space for themselves, both individually and as a couple. It wasn't just about growing the business anymore, it was about living fully and intentionally while doing so.

Principle: The Importance of Time Management and Balance

Kofo and Sunshine's realization that they needed balance came at a critical time in their journey. They had poured everything into **Sellapy** and **SellapyTech**, but they quickly learned that success without balance could lead to burnout, strained relationships, and ultimately, a loss of joy in the process. Here's how they mastered **time management** and **balance** while continuing to grow their company.

1. **Prioritize What Matters Most**: The first step Kofo and Sunshine took was to **redefine their priorities**. They knew that they couldn't do everything, so they began identifying the most important tasks that moved the needle for Sellapy's growth. Instead of trying to manage every little detail, they focused on the **high-impact activities**, the projects and decisions that would drive the company forward. This shift allowed them to work smarter, not harder, and freed up time for personal pursuits.

2. **Delegate and Empower Your Team**: Kofo and Sunshine had always been **hands-on** leaders, but they quickly realized that they couldn't—and shouldn't—do it all themselves. They began delegating more responsibilities to their trusted team members, empowering them to make decisions and drive initiatives forward. By trusting their team and giving them more ownership, Kofo and Sunshine were able to step back from day-to-day operations and focus on higher-level strategy. Delegation wasn't just about offloading tasks, it was about creating **space for balance**.

3. **Set Boundaries Around Work**: One of the most important changes they made was setting **clear boundaries** around work. They established rules for themselves; no emails after 8:00 p.m., no meetings on Sundays, and dedicated time for personal activities. This wasn't easy at first, especially when work felt endless, but it was necessary. By setting boundaries, they protected their time, which helped them recharge and return to work with renewed energy. It also gave them time to nurture their relationship and personal well-being.

4. **Use Time-Blocking for Focus**: Kofo and Sunshine adopted the practice of **time-blocking**, scheduling dedicated blocks of time for specific tasks, projects, and personal activities. This helped them stay focused during work hours and prevented them from getting overwhelmed by multitasking. Time-blocking also ensured that they carved out **non-negotiable time** for personal activities like exercise, date nights, and hobbies. They realized that by structuring their time with intention, they could achieve more in fewer hours and still make time for themselves.

5. **Protect Time for Personal Fulfilment**: Kofo and Sunshine understood that life was about more than just business. They made it a priority to protect time for **personal fulfilment**, whether that meant taking weekend getaways, spending time with friends and family, or pursuing hobbies they loved. This time away from work wasn't a distraction; it was what fuelled their creativity, energy, and passion. They discovered that when they nurtured their personal lives, they became more effective leaders, with clearer minds and renewed motivation.

"True success isn't found in working harder—it's found in living fully and intentionally while achieving your goals."

Part 2: The Shift Toward Balance

Over the next few months, Kofo and Sunshine began implementing these changes in their lives. They structured their days with intentionality, focusing on high-impact work during business hours and protecting their personal time with the same level of commitment.

One Friday afternoon, as Kofo wrapped up a meeting with the marketing team, he glanced at the clock and smiled. For the first time in months, he didn't feel the familiar sense of dread as the weekend approached. Instead of staying late to catch up on emails, he had blocked off the evening to spend with Sunshine. They had planned a quiet dinner, followed by a walk through the park, a small but meaningful break from the chaos of their schedules.

When he arrived home, Sunshine was already waiting, her laptop closed and a glass of wine in hand. **"To balance,"** she said, raising her glass with a smile. Kofo chuckled, joining her in the toast. They were both learning that success wasn't just about working harder, it was about working smarter, and living intentionally along the way.

That evening, as they strolled through the park, they talked about how much had changed since they first started Sellapy. The sleepless nights, the never-ending to-do lists, the constant pressure to grow, it had all been worth it. But now, they were learning that balance was just as important as growth. **Their success wasn't just measured in revenue, it was measured in their ability to live full, meaningful lives** while running a thriving business.

For Kofo and Sunshine, time mastery wasn't just about productivity, it was about creating space for the things that mattered most. They had built Sellapy together, but now, they were building something even more important: a life that was as rich and fulfilling as their business success.

Principle: Balance Is Essential for Sustainable Success

Kofo and Sunshine's journey toward balance teaches us that **time management** and **personal well-being** are essential for sustainable success. They discovered that working non-stop wasn't the answer to growing their business—instead, mastering their time and protecting their personal lives made them more effective leaders and allowed them to build a lasting legacy.

Here's why balance is crucial for long-term success:

1. **Avoiding Burnout Leads to Greater Productivity**: When you're constantly running on empty, your productivity takes a hit. Kofo and Sunshine learned that by setting boundaries and taking time to rest and recharge, they were actually more productive during their work hours. Balance prevents burnout, which means you can sustain your energy and creativity for the long haul.

2. **Balance Enhances Creativity and Problem-Solving**: Taking time away from work allows your mind to rest and **recharge**, which leads to clearer thinking and more creative problem-solving. Some of Kofo and Sunshine's best ideas came during

moments when they were disconnected from work, whether during a walk in the park or over a quiet dinner. Balance gives your brain the space it needs to come up with innovative solutions.

3. **Work-Life Integration Is Key to Personal Fulfilment**: For Kofo and Sunshine, integrating their personal lives into their business journey was key to their overall happiness. They realized that they could be successful entrepreneurs without sacrificing the things they loved, whether that was spending time with each other, traveling, or pursuing personal hobbies. Balance allowed them to find **fulfilment in both work and life**.

4. **Balanced Leaders Inspire Balanced Teams**: As Kofo and Sunshine adopted better time management practices, they noticed a shift in their team as well. They encouraged their employees to take breaks, set boundaries, and prioritize their well-being. This culture of balance not only improved team morale but also increased productivity across the company. Balanced leaders create balanced teams, which leads to sustainable success for the entire organization.

"Mastering time isn't about doing more—it's about making space for what matters most."

Part 3: A Taste of the Billionaire Life – The Private Island Escape

It had been a whirlwind year, full of challenges, growth, and breakthroughs. **Sellapy** and **SellapyTech** were flourishing beyond Kofo and Sunshine's wildest dreams, and they had finally found their rhythm, not just in business, but in life. The balance they had worked so hard to cultivate was paying off. But there was something else they had always talked about, something they had promised each other long ago, back when they were just dreaming of success. They had always envisioned a day when they would celebrate the fruits of their labour, truly savouring the life they had built together.

And now, that day had come.

It started with a surprise from Sunshine. As Kofo finished up a strategy call with one of SellapyTech's newest clients, Sunshine walked into the room holding a small envelope.

"**You're going to want to open this,**" she said, a mischievous smile playing on her lips.

Kofo raised an eyebrow but did as she asked. Inside the envelope were two first-class tickets to a **private island in the Caribbean**. But not just any island, this was a **seven-star, ultra-exclusive island resort** known for hosting some of the world's wealthiest and most influential people. It was a place they had once only **dreamed of visiting**, back when they were bootstrapping their businesses and scraping together resources just to make it through the month.

Now, thanks to their success, that dream had become a reality.

The Billionaire Experience: A Week in Paradise
The moment their plane touched down on the private airstrip, Kofo and Sunshine were greeted by personal attendants who whisked them away in a luxurious yacht to their island villa. It was a scene straight out of a movie, **crystal-clear turquoise waters**, lush greenery, and white sandy beaches stretching as far as the eye could see.

For the first time in a long time, Kofo and Sunshine felt a sense of **total freedom**. There were no deadlines to meet, no meetings to prepare for, just the warm Caribbean breeze and the sound of waves gently lapping against the shore. As they settled into their private villa, complete with infinity pools, personal chefs, and every luxury imaginable, it finally hit them.

"We made it," Kofo said, looking out at the ocean, his voice filled with wonder. Sunshine smiled and took his hand. **"Yes, we did,"** she replied softly.

For the next week, they lived the **billionaire life** they had once only talked about in passing. Every day was filled with moments of pure bliss, whether it was taking a **sunset sail on a private yacht**, enjoying a **five-course dinner** on the beach under the stars, or simply lounging by the pool, completely disconnected from the demands of their busy lives. It wasn't just a vacation; it was the culmination of everything they had worked so hard for.

But beyond the luxury and the relaxation, there was something even more profound happening. Kofo and Sunshine realized that this was more than just a **once-in-**

a-lifetime experience. It was a celebration of their journey, a testament to the **power of their vision** and the **hard work** that had brought them here.

As they strolled along the beach one evening, watching the sun dip below the horizon, Kofo turned to Sunshine and said, **"We should do this every year. A 'save the date' moment, just for us. A reminder that all the hard work, all the sacrifices, it's not just for the business. It's for us, too."**

Sunshine nodded; her eyes sparkling. **"I was thinking the same thing,"** she said. **"A yearly tradition; our time to reconnect, reflect, and enjoy everything we've built together."**

The Annual "Save the Date" Tradition

That evening, they made a pact. Every year, they would return to a place like this; a **luxurious escape**, a week dedicated to themselves, away from the hustle and bustle of running a global business. It would be their **annual 'save the date' tradition**, a celebration of not just their success but of their relationship, their partnership, and the life they had created together.

It wasn't just about indulging in luxury. For Kofo and Sunshine, this yearly retreat represented a **balance of hard work and reward**. It reminded them that the grind, the long nights, the calculated risks. They all had a purpose. And that purpose wasn't just about building a company, it was about building a life of **freedom, joy, and fulfilment**.

During their stay on the island, they also spent time reflecting on their journey. How far they had come, the obstacles they had overcome, and the people they had met along the way. They talked about the future, what they still wanted to achieve, and how they could continue to grow not just as entrepreneurs but as individuals.

By the end of the trip, they were recharged, rejuvenated, and ready to return to the world with **renewed energy and focus**. But now, they had something new to look forward to, a yearly reminder that while **success is hard-earned**, it's also meant to be **enjoyed**.

Principle: Hard Work Pays Off, But Don't Forget to Celebrate

Kofo and Sunshine's private island vacation wasn't just a reward for their hard work, it was a **symbol** of the life they had always envisioned. They had poured their hearts and souls into **Sellapy** and **SellapyTech**, but now they understood the importance of celebrating the fruits of their labour.

Here's what their experience teaches us:

1. **Celebrate Your Wins**: As entrepreneurs, it's easy to get caught up in the grind and forget to celebrate the milestones along the way. Kofo and Sunshine realized that **celebrating success** isn't just a luxury, it's essential. Taking time to acknowledge and enjoy the rewards of your hard work helps you stay motivated and reminds you of why you started in the first place.

2. **Create 'Save the Date' Moments**: Setting aside time each year to disconnect from the daily grind and reconnect with yourself, your partner, or your loved ones is crucial for maintaining balance and perspective. By creating an annual 'save the date' tradition, Kofo and Sunshine ensured that they would always make time for the things that

mattered most, their relationship, their well-being, and their shared vision for the future.

3. **Hard Work Should Lead to Freedom**: Kofo and Sunshine's journey wasn't just about financial success. It was about creating **freedom**. Their time on the island reminded them that the ultimate reward for all their hard work wasn't just money or accolades. It was the freedom to **live life on their terms**. Success should give you the ability to enjoy life, not just work harder.

4. **Dream Big, Then Live It**: The private island vacation was something Kofo and Sunshine had dreamed of for years, but it had once seemed like a distant fantasy. By **dreaming big** and working hard, they turned that dream into reality. Their experience is a reminder that if you have the courage to dream big, and the dedication to pursue it, you can create a life that exceeds your wildest expectations.

Actionable Takeaways

Here are three steps you can take to balance hard work with meaningful celebration and reward:

1. **Identify Your High-Impact Tasks**: Focus on the tasks and activities that have the greatest impact on your business or career. Let go of low-priority tasks that drain your time and energy. By concentrating on what truly matters, you'll accomplish more in less time.
2. **Set Boundaries Around Work**: Establish clear boundaries for your workday. Decide on a time to stop working each day, and stick to it. Schedule dedicated time for personal activities, and treat it as non-negotiable. Protecting your personal time is key to maintaining a healthy balance.
3. **Integrate Personal Fulfilment into Your Routine**: Make time for the things that bring you joy and fulfilment outside of work. Whether it's spending time with loved ones, pursuing hobbies, or simply taking time to rest, personal fulfilment fuels long-term success. When you're happy and balanced, you bring more energy and creativity to your work.

4. **Plan Your Own "Save the Date" Tradition**: Whether it's an annual vacation, a weekend getaway, or a day of celebration, make it a point to set aside time each year to **celebrate your wins**. Use this time to reflect on your journey, recharge, and enjoy the fruits of your labour.
5. **Visualize the Life You Want to Live**: Take time to think about the kind of life you want to create through your hard work. It's not just about financial success. It's about the **experiences and freedom** you want to enjoy. Keep that vision in mind as you work, and let it fuel your motivation.
6. **Balance Success with Enjoyment**: As you achieve success, make sure you're also taking time to **enjoy** it. Success without joy is empty. Make space in your life for celebration, relaxation, and the things that bring you happiness.

For Kofo and Sunshine, their private island vacation marked the beginning of a new chapter, not just as business leaders, but as **visionaries living the life they had always dreamed of.** Their story is a powerful reminder that hard work and smart decisions do pay off, and when they do, you owe it to yourself to **live fully and intentionally**.

"The greatest reward for hard work isn't just success— it's the freedom to live the life you once dreamed of."

In the next chapter, we'll explore how Kofo and Sunshine navigated the challenges of **embracing change and disruption**, ensuring that Sellapy and SellapyTech remained at the forefront of innovation, even in an unpredictable world.

Chapter 9

Embracing Change and Disruption

Part 1: The Disruption That Nearly Derailed It All

The email came early on a Monday morning. Kofo was just sitting down with his coffee when he saw the subject line: **"Urgent: Regulatory Changes Impacting International Shipping for Small Businesses."** His stomach tightened as he clicked to open the message.

Sellapy had been thriving, with thousands of vendors using the platform to reach global customers. But now, a new set of **regulatory changes** threatened to disrupt everything. Governments in key markets had imposed stricter regulations on **international shipping** for small businesses, making it more expensive and complicated for vendors to send their products across borders. This wasn't just a minor obstacle, if Sellapy didn't adapt, they could lose a significant portion of their vendor base, especially those in emerging markets.

Kofo sat back in his chair, his mind racing. He knew that this could either be a devastating setback or an opportunity for Sellapy to innovate. The answer would depend on how quickly they could **adapt.**

Sunshine, always one step ahead, entered the office a few minutes later. She had received the same email. **"We need to pivot fast,"** she said, her voice calm but determined. **"This could affect thousands of our vendors if we don't find a solution."**

Kofo nodded. **"This is disruption,"** he said. **"But we've faced worse before. We just need to figure out how to turn it into an opportunity."**

They immediately called an emergency meeting with their leadership team. Over the next few hours, they brainstormed solutions, analysed the new regulations, and mapped out a strategy. But what struck Kofo most was how his team responded, not with panic, but with **creativity and determination**. It was clear that the **culture of innovation and agility** they had fostered over the years was paying off. The team didn't see the disruption as a crisis—they saw it as a chance to lead the market in a new direction.

Principle: How to Turn Disruption Into Opportunity

Kofo and Sunshine's ability to **embrace disruption** and adapt quickly was one of the key reasons Sellapy and SellapyTech continued to thrive in an ever-changing marketplace. Here's how they turned challenges into opportunities and used **disruption** as a tool for innovation:

1. **Accept That Change Is Inevitable**: The first step in dealing with disruption is **acceptance**. Kofo and Sunshine didn't waste time lamenting the regulatory changes or wishing things would go back to normal. They understood that change is a constant in business, and the sooner you accept it, the sooner you can start adapting. Instead of fighting the disruption, they leaned into it, looking for ways to turn it to their advantage.

2. **See Disruption as an Opportunity for Innovation**: Kofo and Sunshine had always believed that **disruption breeds innovation**.

The new regulations were a setback, but they also opened the door for new ideas. By embracing the challenge, they were able to come up with innovative solutions that not only addressed the immediate issue but also gave Sellapy a competitive advantage. They saw the disruption as an opportunity to **improve their platform** and strengthen their relationship with vendors.

3. **Be Agile and Act Quickly**: One of the most important aspects of dealing with disruption is **speed**. Kofo and Sunshine didn't sit around waiting for the situation to resolve itself, they acted quickly. They mobilized their team, gathered information, and put a plan in place within days. This agility allowed Sellapy to stay ahead of the curve and avoid the potential fallout that could have come from inaction. In a world of constant change, **speed is essential**.

4. **Communicate and Reassure Your Team and Stakeholders**: During times of disruption, **clear communication** is key. Kofo and Sunshine made sure their team was informed every step of the way. They also communicated openly with their vendors, letting them know that Sellapy was working on

solutions to navigate the new regulations. By keeping everyone in the loop, they maintained trust and kept the lines of communication open, which helped reduce panic and uncertainty.

"The greatest challenge in disruption is not surviving the storm—it's finding the opportunity hidden in its chaos."

Part 2: The Pivot That Saved the Day

After hours of brainstorming, the solution finally emerged. Instead of trying to work around the new regulations, Kofo and Sunshine decided to **partner with local logistics companies** in key markets. These companies could navigate the regulatory complexities more efficiently than global shipping providers, offering local solutions to Sellapy's vendors. The pivot allowed Sellapy to **absorb some of the extra costs** on behalf of their vendors while also ensuring that products could still reach international customers without major delays.

But that wasn't the only pivot. Sunshine suggested that they use this disruption as an opportunity to **promote local trade**, encouraging vendors to target customers within their own regions, minimising the need for international shipping altogether. By adding features to the platform that highlighted local buyers, Sellapy could help vendors expand their customer base **locally and globally**, making them less dependent on international shipping.

The team immediately got to work. Within weeks, they had launched the new local logistics partnerships and added the **"Local Buyer" feature** to the platform, allowing vendors to target customers closer to home. The results were remarkable. Vendors appreciated Sellapy's swift response and the new tools, and many found that their local sales surged, reducing their reliance on international markets.

The regulatory changes that had once seemed like a threat had become an **opportunity** for Sellapy to diversify its offerings and strengthen its value proposition to vendors.

Principle: Adaptability Is Key to Long-Term Success

The ability to **adapt to change** is one of the most critical factors in long-term success. For Kofo and Sunshine, embracing disruption wasn't just a survival tactic, it was a competitive advantage. Here's how adaptability can ensure your business thrives, even in the face of major challenges:

1. **Be Willing to Pivot**: Kofo and Sunshine's success wasn't just about reacting to disruption, it was about being willing to **pivot** their strategy when necessary. They didn't cling to old models that no longer worked; they were open to new ideas and approaches. Flexibility is key when dealing with disruption, those who can pivot quickly are more likely to come out ahead.

2. **Innovation Is a Continuous Process**: One of the lessons Kofo and Sunshine learned was that **innovation never stops**. The best businesses are always looking for ways to improve, even when things are going well. By fostering a culture of continuous innovation, they were able to come up with creative solutions to the regulatory challenge and keep Sellapy moving forward.

3. **Focus on Customer Needs**: Throughout the disruption, Kofo and Sunshine kept their focus on

what mattered most, the needs of their vendors and customers. By listening to their vendors' concerns and finding ways to alleviate the impact of the new regulations, they strengthened their relationships and increased loyalty. In times of disruption, staying close to your customers' needs is essential for long-term success.

4. **Stay Positive and Forward-Thinking**: Finally, Kofo and Sunshine's **mindset** was critical to their ability to navigate disruption. They didn't let fear or uncertainty derail them. Instead, they approached the challenge with a **positive, forward-thinking attitude**, believing that they could turn the situation to their advantage. Maintaining a positive outlook is key to finding solutions and keeping your team motivated in times of change.

"Adaptability isn't just about adjusting to change—it's about using change to propel you forward."

Part 3: Sellapy's Disruptive Innovation

Kofo and Sunshine's success in navigating the regulatory disruption wasn't the only time they turned a challenge into an opportunity. Throughout their journey, they continually embraced disruption as a tool for innovation. Whether it was adopting **AI technology** to streamline operations or using **business credit** to fuel rapid growth, they were never afraid to take risks or push the boundaries of what was possible.

One of the most disruptive innovations they introduced was the launch of **SellapyTech**. As the eCommerce space evolved, they saw that businesses were struggling to keep up with the demands of automation, AI, and data analytics. Instead of staying solely focused on Sellapy's marketplace, they decided to launch **SellapyTech** as a separate company, offering **AI-powered solutions** to other businesses in need of advanced technology.

The move was risky, but it paid off. SellapyTech quickly became a **multi-million-pound subsidiary**, helping companies around the world integrate AI into their operations. What had once been a side project became a disruptive force in the tech industry, and it positioned Kofo and Sunshine as **leaders in both eCommerce and AI**.

Actionable Takeaways

Here are three steps you can take to embrace change and turn disruption into opportunity:

1. **Anticipate and Prepare for Disruption**: Disruption is inevitable, but it doesn't have to catch you off guard. Stay informed about changes in your industry, technology, and market trends. By **anticipating disruption**, you can prepare and respond proactively, rather than reactively.

2. **Encourage a Culture of Innovation**: Foster a culture where **innovation is continuous**. Encourage your team to experiment with new ideas and approaches, even when things are going well. When disruption happens, an innovative mindset will help you find creative solutions quickly.

3. **Focus on the Opportunity Within the Challenge**:
Every disruption presents an opportunity for growth and innovation. Instead of viewing

challenges as setbacks, look for the **opportunities hidden within**. Whether it's a new market, a chance to improve processes, or a way to introduce a new product, disruption can be the catalyst for your next big move.

Kofo and Sunshine's ability to embrace change and turn disruption into opportunity was one of the keys to their success. They didn't just react to the challenges they faced—they **innovated through them**, ensuring that Sellapy and SellapyTech remained ahead of the curve in an ever-changing marketplace.

"Disruption isn't a threat—it's an invitation to innovate and lead the market in a new direction."

In the final chapter, we'll explore how Kofo and Sunshine built a **lasting legacy**, ensuring that their impact would go beyond their businesses and continue to influence future generations.

Chapter 10

Creating a Lasting Legacy

Part 1: The Legacy Conversation That Changed Everything

It was a quiet afternoon in the garden of their London home when Kofo and Sunshine found themselves reflecting on their journey. They had built **Sellapy** and **SellapyTech** into thriving, multi-million-pound businesses. They had navigated challenges, embraced change, and enjoyed the rewards of their hard work. But now, as they sat together, the question that had been lingering in Kofo's mind finally surfaced.

"What happens after this?" he asked, his voice thoughtful. "What happens when we're no longer running things day to day? What do we leave behind?"

Sunshine looked at him, her eyes filled with the same deep thought. **"I've been thinking about that too,"** she admitted. **"We've created something incredible, but the real question is: how do we make sure it lasts? How do we ensure that our impact goes beyond just us?"**

The conversation marked the beginning of a **new chapter** in their lives. While they had always focused on building their businesses and growing their brands, Kofo and Sunshine realized that the **true measure of their success** would be the **legacy** they left behind, the impact that would endure long after they stepped away from the day-to-day operations.

They knew that legacy wasn't just about wealth or business, it was about creating a lasting impact on the lives of others, the communities they served, and the industries they transformed. And now, it was time to shift their focus from growth to **sustainability, mentorship, and giving back.**

Principle: Building a Legacy That Lasts Beyond Success

For Kofo and Sunshine, building a legacy wasn't about ensuring their names would be remembered. It was about creating something that would continue to **empower, inspire, and uplift** others. Here's how they approached the task of building a lasting legacy:

1. **Mentorship and Empowerment**: One of the first steps they took was to **mentor the next generation of entrepreneurs**. Kofo and Sunshine had always believed in the power of small businesses and innovation, and they wanted to ensure that their journey could inspire others to pursue their own dreams. They began hosting **entrepreneurship workshops**, sharing their knowledge, experiences, and lessons learned with young innovators from around the world. By **empowering others** with the tools and guidance they had wished for in their early days, Kofo and Sunshine created a ripple effect of impact.

"Our success doesn't end with us," Sunshine said during their first mentorship session. **"It continues in the lives we touch and the dreams we help others achieve."**

2. **Creating a Culture of Innovation**: For Kofo and Sunshine, legacy also meant creating a business culture that would **thrive without them**. They worked hard to build **Sellapy** and **SellapyTech** into companies that could innovate and grow even after they stepped back from leadership. They empowered their **management teams** to carry the torch, fostering a culture of continuous improvement and ethical business practices. This meant creating a structure where **employees were not just workers but innovators,** able to adapt to the changing marketplace and continue driving the company forward.

3. **Giving Back Through Philanthropy**: As they reflected on their journey, Kofo and Sunshine also felt a deep desire to give back to the communities that had supported their growth. They established the **Sellapy Foundation**, a philanthropic organization dedicated to **supporting small businesses in developing countries**, providing

them with access to technology, funding, and education. Their foundation focused on creating **lasting impact** through social entrepreneurship, ethical business practices, and community-driven innovation.

Kofo and Sunshine had always believed in using business as a force for good, and the **Sellapy Foundation** was the ultimate manifestation of that belief. By funding **micro-loans** for small business owners in underserved communities, they ensured that their legacy wasn't just about business success—it was about **changing lives**.

4. **Sustainability and Ethical Business**: From the very beginning, Kofo and Sunshine had emphasized the importance of **ethical and sustainable business practices**. They knew that for their legacy to last, they had to prioritize **sustainability**, not just for their businesses, but for the environment and society as a whole. They integrated sustainability into the core of Sellapy's operations, from sourcing eco-friendly products to promoting fair trade practices across the marketplace.

"We didn't build Sellapy to just succeed in business," Kofo often said. **"We built it to leave the world a little better than we found it."**

"True legacy isn't measured by what you leave behind—it's measured by the lives you've touched along the way."

Part 2: The Moment of Stepping Back

The day finally came when Kofo and Sunshine decided it was time to **step back** from the daily grind of running Sellapy and SellapyTech. They had groomed a strong leadership team, put processes in place to ensure the companies would continue to thrive, and set up their philanthropic ventures to give back to the communities they cared about.

As they prepared to leave the office for the last time as the active leaders of the businesses they had built, Kofo and Sunshine stood in the familiar conference room where so many ideas had been born, deals had been made, and challenges had been overcome. The walls were filled with pictures and memories from their journey, a reminder of the **impact** they had made.

"**This is just the beginning,**" Sunshine said softly, turning to Kofo. "**The legacy we've built will continue long after we're gone.**"

Kofo smiled, feeling a deep sense of peace. "**We've done what we set out to do,**" he replied. "**Now it's time to let the legacy carry itself forward.**"

They left the building hand in hand, ready to enjoy the next chapter of their lives, one filled with more time for personal fulfilment, family, and new adventures. But as they walked away, they knew that the **work they had done**, the businesses they had built, the people they had mentored, the lives they had touched, would live on.

Principle: Legacy Is About More Than Success

Kofo and Sunshine understood that **true legacy** isn't just about the wealth or businesses you leave behind. It's about the **impact you create**, the people you empower, and the values you instil. Here's what they learned about building a legacy that lasts:

1. **Your Legacy Lives in the People You Empower**: Kofo and Sunshine knew that their

greatest legacy wasn't the companies they had built. It was the **people they had empowered** along the way. Whether through mentorship, leadership development, or philanthropy, they made it their mission to uplift others, ensuring that their impact would continue through the lives of the people they had touched.

2. **Legacy Is Built on Values, Not Just Success**: For Kofo and Sunshine, legacy wasn't just about financial success. It was about the **values** they had instilled in their businesses and communities. By prioritizing ethical business practices, sustainability, and empowerment, they ensured that the companies they built would continue to operate in alignment with their core beliefs.

3. **Give Back, and Your Legacy Will Grow**: The **Sellapy Foundation** was a testament to Kofo and Sunshine's belief in **giving back**. They understood that true legacy isn't just about what you achieve for yourself. It's about how you use your success to lift others. By investing in communities and social entrepreneurship, they created a legacy that would grow far beyond their own lifetimes.

4. **Legacy Is About Creating Something That Lasts**: Ultimately, Kofo and Sunshine's legacy wasn't just about the businesses they built. It was about **creating something that would last**. They focused on building systems, empowering leaders, and instilling a culture of innovation that would allow Sellapy and SellapyTech to continue thriving without them.

Kofo and Sunshine's journey to create a lasting legacy is a testament to the power of **empowerment, values, and giving back**. They built more than just businesses, they built a legacy that would continue to **inspire, empower, and uplift** others for generations to come.

As they stepped back from their companies, they knew their impact wouldn't end. It was just beginning. Their story reminds us that success is only the beginning of a true legacy, what matters most is the **impact you leave behind**.

"Success fades, but a legacy built on values and empowerment lasts forever."

Part 3: The Philanthropy Plan That Touched Millions

It was a conversation that had been years in the making. As **Kofo** and **Sunshine** stood overlooking the fertile lands of their newly acquired property in rural Nigeria, they knew that this would be their most important legacy yet. The rolling green hills stretched far into the distance, and the sun bathed the earth with a warm golden glow. This wasn't just land. It was a promise, a **vision** for the future, and the beginning of their most ambitious project yet: **Sellapy Farms**.

For years, Kofo and Sunshine had dedicated their lives to building Sellapy and SellapyTech, empowering small businesses, and using technology to uplift the global marketplace. But now, their focus had shifted to something even closer to their hearts: **feeding the poorest, empowering local farmers, and creating a sustainable future for Africa's communities**.

Kofo, with his background as an **Economist**, had long been fascinated by the idea of reshaping the economic models that had failed the poorest communities. He had always believed that the answer wasn't just about injecting money into economies. It was about **rethinking the systems** that kept people in poverty. Sunshine, a **nurse** and **mental health counsellor**, had seen first-hand the effects of **poverty, hunger, and mental health struggles** in the communities she worked with. For her, this wasn't just an economic issue it was about **restoring dignity, hope, and mental well-being** to those who had been forgotten.

Together, they envisioned a future where Sellapy Farms would not only feed the hungry but also create a **sustainable model** of agriculture that could be replicated across Africa, restoring balance and peace to the communities they served.

The Vision: Sellapy Farms and the New Barter System

Sellapy Farms wasn't going to be just another charity project. Kofo and Sunshine had a **radical vision** for how the farm would operate, one rooted in the **ancient practice of barter**, where communities could trade goods and services without relying solely on money. They believed that **money** had become a **curse** for many of the world's poorest communities, draining economies and fracturing mental health. The pursuit of cash flow had led to exploitation, stress, and a growing sense of despair among those who could never seem to earn enough to survive.

Kofo had spent years studying how **modern economies** had left rural farmers behind, trapping them in cycles of debt and dependency on external forces. Sunshine, in her role as a mental health counsellor, had witnessed the **emotional toll** this financial strain took on families, contributing to **anxiety, depression, and hopelessness**. Together, they envisioned a model that would free local farmers from this crushing burden.

Sellapy Farms would function as a **barter-based agricultural community**, where farmers could trade their crops, skills, and services with one another, creating a **self-sustaining economy** that didn't rely on cash. This model would allow farmers to trade surplus food for tools, education for their children, healthcare, or other essentials, all without the pressure of earning money in a system designed to keep them impoverished.

But it wasn't just about the barter system. Kofo and Sunshine envisioned Sellapy Farms as a place where the **poorest of the poor** would receive **three meals a day**, nourishing not just their bodies, but their **spirits and mental well-being**. For Sunshine, this wasn't just about food security, it was about **healing communities** from the inside out.

"We've spent our lives building businesses," Sunshine said one evening as they discussed their plans. **"Now, it's time to build something that feeds the soul, something that brings peace to those who have lived in fear and hunger for too long."**

Kofo nodded. His economist mind was already calculating the logistics, but this project wasn't just about numbers—it was about creating a **new model of hope**. **"We're not just feeding people,"** he said. **"We're restoring their dignity, their pride, their ability to stand on their own two feet. The world doesn't need more charity. It needs a new way of thinking, a system that works for everyone, not just those at the top."**

The Old Meets New: Barter, Sustainability, and Mental Health

Sellapy Farms would become a **symbol of what could be achieved** when modern thinking met ancient wisdom. The barter system would allow farmers to **reclaim their power**, trading crops and services without needing to rely on cash in a market that often worked against them. Kofo and Sunshine's vision was to create an **ecosystem** where food, education, healthcare, and community would be traded as valuable currencies.

To ensure the farm's sustainability, they planned to incorporate **modern agricultural techniques** alongside traditional methods. They would introduce **solar-powered irrigation systems**, **organic farming practices**, and **community-driven technology**, all aimed at ensuring that Sellapy Farms would be a **model of sustainability** for generations to come.

But Sunshine's focus wasn't just on the physical. As a mental health counsellor, she knew that feeding people's bodies wouldn't be enough if their minds remained in turmoil. She envisioned **mental health services** being integrated into Sellapy Farms **counselling sessions**,

group therapy, and wellness programs designed to help people heal from the trauma of poverty and hunger.

"This farm will be more than just a place for food," she said passionately during one of their planning meetings. "It will be a place of healing, where people can recover not only their strength but their sense of purpose. We need to give them more than just food—we need to give them back their peace of mind."

The Long-Term Plan: Creating Generational Change

Kofo and Sunshine didn't want Sellapy Farms to be a short-term solution. They envisioned it as a **model that could be replicated across Africa**, a blueprint for how communities could break free from the limitations of cash economies, reconnect with sustainable agriculture, and create their own **self-sufficient ecosystems**. They dreamed of **Sellapy Farms** becoming a network, spanning across countries, empowering local farmers, and providing food security for millions.

Kofo, always the strategist, saw this as the ultimate test of his economic theories. **"If we can prove that this works, that barter and community-driven economies can thrive, we could change the entire landscape of poverty in Africa,"** he explained. **"We could show the world that there's a way out of the cycle of debt and dependency."**

Sunshine, ever the compassionate soul, saw it from a more emotional perspective. **"We're not just changing economies,"** she said. **"We're changing lives. We're helping people rediscover hope, helping children grow up without hunger, helping mothers and fathers feel like they can provide again."**

They knew that the work wouldn't be easy, but they were driven by a deep sense of purpose. This wasn't just a business venture or a philanthropic project, it was their **life's work**, the culmination of everything they believed in. Sellapy Farms would be their **final legacy**, a gift to the people of Africa and the world.

Principle: Legacy Through Sustainable Impact

Kofo and Sunshine's vision for Sellapy Farms wasn't just about feeding people. It was about **changing the way communities lived and thrived**. Here's what their philanthropic plan teaches us:

1. **Empower People to Build Their Own Future**: Kofo and Sunshine believed that true philanthropy wasn't about giving handouts, it was about giving people the tools and systems to **build their own future**. Sellapy Farms would empower local farmers to trade, grow, and sustain their communities without relying on external forces.

2. **Integrate Mental Health and Well-Being**: Sunshine's background in mental health shaped their approach to philanthropy. They understood that feeding the body was important, but feeding the **mind and soul** was just as essential. Their farm would provide **holistic care**, addressing both the physical and emotional needs of the people they served.

3. **Sustainability Is Key to Long-Term Impact**: Kofo and Sunshine designed Sellapy Farms with **sustainability** at its core. They knew that for their legacy to last, the farm had to be self-sufficient,

using modern agricultural techniques and community-driven systems to ensure long-term success. Their vision was to create a **model that could be replicated**, changing not just individual lives but entire communities.

4. **Philanthropy Should Create Systems, Not Dependence**: Kofo's economic background taught him that true impact comes from **building systems**, not creating dependency. The barter system at Sellapy Farms would allow communities to thrive without relying on cash economies, creating **generational change** and breaking the cycle of poverty.

Actionable Takeaways

Here are six steps you can take to create a philanthropic legacy with long-lasting impact:

1. **Empower Others Along the Way**: Your legacy lives in the people you touch and empower. Whether through mentorship, leadership development, or philanthropy, focus on empowering others to succeed. The impact you create through others will outlast your individual success.
2. **Lead with Values**: Your legacy is built on the **values** you bring to your business and your life. Whether it's ethical business practices, sustainability, or community support, make sure your values are at the core of everything you do. This will ensure your legacy is meaningful and lasting.
3. **Give Back and Invest in the Future**: A lasting legacy is built through **giving back**. Invest in the future by supporting causes that matter to you, creating opportunities for others, and using your success to uplift communities. Your legacy will grow as you give back to the world around you.
4. **Think Beyond Charity, Build Systems**: True philanthropy isn't just about giving—it's about **building systems** that empower people to sustain

themselves. Focus on creating models that can thrive long after you're gone.

5. **Address Both Physical and Mental Needs**: When creating impact, don't just focus on the **physical needs** of those you serve. Address mental health and emotional well-being as part of your philanthropic plan. Healing the whole person creates more lasting change.

6. **Incorporate Sustainability into Your Vision**: Build sustainability into the core of your legacy. Whether it's through environmental practices, economic systems, or community-driven solutions, ensuring that your impact is sustainable is key to long-term success.

As Kofo and Sunshine stood at the edge of Sellapy Farms, watching the sunset over the land they would soon transform, they knew that this was more than just a farm. It was their **final, lasting gift** to the world. A legacy of empowerment, healing, and sustainable change. They had built businesses, changed lives, and now they were going to feed not just bodies, but **souls**.

Adegbuyi Oduguwa

"The greatest legacy isn't found in wealth or buildings, it's found in the hearts of the people you feed, heal, and empower to thrive without you."

The Final Revelation: A Vision from the Present into the Future

I stand here today, not just as the founder of **Sellapy**, **SellapyTech**, and the dreamer behind **Sellapy Farms**, but as a reflection of the journey that countless young entrepreneurs like myself arere on right now. This story I've shared with you is more than just a fictional narrative; it's a vision of what's possible when **ambition, resilience, and purpose** come together. It's a story rooted in the heart of someone who refused to be limited by circumstances and dared to dream beyond borders, from **London to Nigeria**, and beyond.

When I started this journey, I was simply a young man, filled with hopes, uncertainty, and a burning desire to **make an impact**. In Kofo's story, I see the struggle of those who start with nothing but ambition, who face rejection, failure, and doubt at every corner, yet keep pushing forward. **Kofo is me, Kofo is you**, and Kofo is everyone who has ever had a dream so big that the world couldn't help but take notice.

Through **Sellapy**, I wanted to create a **marketplace of opportunity**, a platform where the smallest of businesses could dream just as big as the largest corporations. Through **SellapyTech**, I saw the potential to not only build for the present but to help others harness the power of **technology and AI** for a future that doesn't leave anyone behind. And through **Sellapy Farms**, I envision a world where hunger is a distant memory, where the poorest are not forgotten, but empowered to thrive through **sustainable, community-driven systems**.

This journey hasn't been easy. There have been moments of self-doubt, moments when it seemed like the dream was too far to reach. But every step of the way, **Sunshine**, my partner, my inestimable sweetie pie stood beside me. Together, we built not just businesses, but a vision of a better world, one where **entrepreneurship meets compassion** and success is measured not just by profit, but by **the lives we uplift**.

Our story is one of building an empire, not for ourselves, but for those who have been overlooked, for the small business owners, the farmers, the artisans, and for every person who believes that **success should be shared**.

I wrote this story because I believe in the power of storytelling to change minds, ignite passions, and **inspire action**. My goal isn't just to tell you what I've done, it's to show you that **you can do it too**. Whether you're a young entrepreneur starting out with nothing but a dream, or someone looking for the next way to make a difference in the world, I want this book to serve as a **roadmap**. I want you to see yourself in Kofo's story, to recognize the challenges and the triumphs, and to know that no matter where you start, you can create something **extraordinary**.

And now, I turn to **you**, the reader. As much as this is my story, it's also **your story**. The vision I have for the future of **Sellapy Farms**, of a world where sustainable commerce lifts entire communities, is something we can only build **together**. I'm not just asking for your support; I'm asking for your **belief in this vision**. Imagine a world where **local farmers**, who have been trapped in cycles of poverty, can trade through a **barter system** that frees them from the chains of debt. Imagine a world where businesses across the globe are empowered by technology, and where **success** is no longer hoarded by the few, but shared among the many.

This is the future I see. It's not just fiction, it's **our reality in the making**. And together, we can bring it to life.

I invite you to join me and Sunshine in building this future. We've laid the groundwork, but this vision is far bigger than the two of us. Whether you're an entrepreneur, an investor, a philanthropist, or simply someone who believes that the world can be **a better place**, your role in this story is just beginning.

Let's dream big. Let's build an empire, not of wealth alone, but of **impact**. Let's create a legacy that lasts far beyond our lifetimes, one that **empowers the poor**, heals the broken, and gives **everyone a seat at the table**.

This is the story of Kofo and Sunshine, but it's also **your story**. The world we want is within our reach, and together, we can make it happen.

Welcome to the vision. Welcome to the future. Let's build it together.

Summary of the Chapters

Chapter 1: The Ambition Blueprint

Kofo's journey begins in **Nigeria**, where he rises from a **disadvantaged background** to become a successful entrepreneur. Despite immense challenges, he embraces his hidden ambition, works as a labourer in London, and eventually transitions into IT. From there, he bootstraps his way into entrepreneurship, launching **Sellapy** to empower small businesses globally. The chapter focuses on discovering your personal "why," setting audacious goals, and building a blueprint for success.

Chapter 2: The Power of Mindset

This chapter introduces Kofo's shift from a **fixed mindset** to a **growth mindset** after facing failure and rejection. Instead of accepting defeat, Kofo reinvents himself, learning from mistakes and developing the resilience to persist through adversity. His journey highlights the importance of overcoming limiting beliefs and adopting a mindset of continuous learning and growth, showing how the right mindset shapes success.

Chapter 3: Turning Failure into Innovation

Kofo's early failures with **Sellapy's initial iterations** targeting micro businesses and eco-friendly products turned into pivotal moments for innovation. After each setback, Kofo pivots the business, learns valuable lessons, and ultimately repositions Sellapy as a global marketplace for SMEs. Failure becomes the foundation for success, showing that innovation often emerges from adversity and mistakes.

Chapter 4: Leading with Purpose

Kofo transforms from an entrepreneur into a **purpose-driven leader**. He realigns Sellapy's mission, ensuring that every employee, vendor, and customer understands the platform's goal of empowering small businesses and promoting ethical commerce. Leadership isn't just about driving profits—it's about creating a shared vision that resonates with your team and community, inspiring long-term success rooted in purpose.

Chapter 5: Strategic Risk-Taking for Growth

Kofo and Sunshine decide to take bold, calculated risks, using **business credit** and other people's money to invest in **AI infrastructure** and scale Sellapy globally. This risky leap pays off, leading to massive growth. The chapter underscores the importance of **strategic risk-taking**, showing that sometimes, the greatest risk is playing it safe. By leveraging innovation and funding wisely, Kofo and Sunshine unlock new levels of success, including launching **SellapyTech**, a tech subsidiary that helps other businesses thrive.

Chapter 6: The Art of Influence and Persuasion

Kofo and Sunshine use **influence and strategic persuasion** to form key partnerships that drive Sellapy's success. They secure deals with major logistics and fintech companies by focusing on long-term relationships and shared visions, rather than just financial terms. This chapter emphasizes the power of negotiation, showing how building **mutually beneficial relationships** and selling a compelling vision can elevate your business beyond the competition.

Chapter 7: Building High-Performing Teams

As Sellapy grows, Kofo and Sunshine transition from hands-on entrepreneurs to leaders of a **high-performing team**. They empower their employees to take ownership of the company's mission, creating a culture of collaboration and innovation. This chapter focuses on the importance of fostering teamwork, recognizing contributions, and empowering teams to drive the company's success independently.

Chapter 8: Time Mastery and Balance

Kofo and Sunshine face the pressure of running a global company while maintaining a **healthy work-life balance**. They learn to prioritize tasks, delegate responsibilities, and set boundaries around work. This chapter highlights the importance of mastering time and protecting personal fulfilment, showing that balance is key to sustaining long-term success without burnout.

Chapter 9: Embracing Change and Disruption

Sellapy faces regulatory changes that threaten to disrupt its operations, but Kofo and Sunshine **pivot quickly**, forming new logistics partnerships and embracing innovation to overcome the challenge. They view disruption as an opportunity for growth, reinforcing that adaptability and quick decision-making are critical in a constantly evolving marketplace. This chapter emphasizes the importance of turning disruption into opportunity by staying agile and innovative.

Chapter 10: Creating a Lasting Legacy

Kofo and Sunshine begin focusing on their **legacy**, establishing **Sellapy Farms**, a sustainable initiative to feed the poorest communities in Africa. The farm introduces a **barter system** that allows farmers to trade goods and services without relying on money, addressing poverty and mental health issues simultaneously. This chapter explores how Kofo's economics background and Sunshine's passion for mental health converge to create a philanthropic project that leaves a lasting impact beyond their businesses. Their legacy is built on **empowerment**, **sustainability**, and giving back to the communities they care about.

Acknowledgements

First and foremost, I give all thanks to **God Almighty** for His grace, guidance, and countless blessings throughout this journey. Without His divine hand, none of this would have been possible.

To my **late father, Chief Kofoworola Oduguwa**, your wisdom, strength, and legacy have been a constant source of inspiration. Though you are no longer with us, your values and teachings continue to guide every step I take. I hope this book honours the incredible path you paved for us. To my dearest **mother, Mrs. B.T. Oduguwa**, your unyielding love, support, and prayers have been the foundation upon which I've built my dreams. You are the heart and soul of our family.

To my brother, **Dr. Adedara Oduguwa**, your brilliance and unwavering belief in me have pushed me to achieve more than I could have imagined. And to my siblings, **Dr. Adebanke**, **Mrs. Adesewa**, and **Mr. Adekoyejo**—thank you for your continued love, encouragement, and support through this entire journey.

Lastly, to my **Sunshine, Oluwatumininu Olagbegi**, the love of my life and my supporter of inestimable value: you are my rock, my greatest fan, and my source of endless inspiration. Your unwavering belief in my dreams, your constant encouragement, and your boundless love have been the wind beneath my wings. Together, we have built something extraordinary, and with you by my side, I know the journey ahead will be even more remarkable.

This book, and all that it stands for, is as much yours as it is mine. Thank you for being my sunshine in every sense of the word.

Adegbuyi Oduguwa

Legacy Makers

Transforming Dreams into Empires that Empower the World

www.ingramcontent.com/pod-product-compliance
Lightning Source LLC
Chambersburg PA
CBHW052158220526
45471CB00004B/1724